HOW TO
CHANGE
YOUR LIFE

HOW TO
CHANGE
YOUR LIFE
FROM THOUGHT TO ACTION

ANTONY KIDMAN

**KOGAN
PAGE**

To Janelle, Nicole and Antonia

First published in Australia in 1988 by
Biochemical & General Services, PO Box 156,
St Leonards, NSW, Australia 2065.

This edition first published in Great Britain
in 1990 by Kogan Page Limited,
120 Pentonville Road, London N1 9JN.

British Library Cataloguing in Publication Data

Kidman, Antony D.
  How to change your life:
  from thought to action
  1. Self-development
  I. Title
  158'.1

  ISBN 1-85091-941-0
  ISBN 1-85091-942-9 Pbk

Typeset by DP Photosetting, Aylesbury, Bucks
Printed and bound in Great Britain by
Biddles Ltd, Guildford

Contents

Foreword

Antony Kidman's *How To Change Your Life* is a book that puts some of the main principles of rational-emotive therapy (RET) into unusually clear action language. As Dr Kidman correctly points out, although RET is noted for helping people to change their disordered feelings, it is also highly behavioural and invariably includes activity homework assignments.

As I note in my forthcoming book, *How to Stubbornly Refuse to Make Yourself Miserable About Anything – Yes, Anything!*, RET provides people with three main insights:

1. You mainly create your own emotional disturbances by the irrational ideas that you tell yourself.
2. No matter when you started to have problems, if you are upset today, you are still believing some dogmatic irrational ideas.
3. To eliminate your anxiety, loneliness, depression and rage, there is no way but work and practice – yes, work and practice.

Dr. Kidman particularly emphasises acting on your newly acquired rational beliefs in this book; and if you follow his practical exercises, you will most probably help yourself to lead a less anxious, less lonely, more organised and happier existence. No guarantees, of course. But try it and see!

Albert Ellis, PhD,
Executive Director,
Institute for Rational-Emotive Therapy, New York

How To Change Your Life is a compendium of the essential self-help techniques of the cognitive-behavioural therapies. Clear, simple instructions and matter-of-fact presentation should make Dr Kidman's book a versatile resource for people who are just not managing their lives as well as they would like, as well as for people suffering from anxiety, depression, loneliness or chronic frustration. The section on self-organisation will help executives and housewives to tackle problems and use time more efficiently. Therapists, too, will learn from Dr Kidman's book and will want to recommend it to clients as a supplement to therapy. All around, *How To Change Your Life* is a welcome contribution to self-help literature.

Aaron T Beck, MD,
Professor of Psychiatry,
University of Pennsylvania

Preface

Following the publication of my first book, *Tactics for Changing Your Life*, I decided to follow this with another that would cover some new topics in greater depth, again concentrating on negative emotions and ways to handle them. In the cognitive behavioural therapeutic model, thoughts lead to feelings and consequent actions, and I decided to concentrate in the first section of this book on feelings and how to dispute negative thoughts, focusing on anxiety and loneliness.

The last section of the book is devoted to action and planning. It is clear, in the persuasive, direct psychotherapeutic approach advocated by Albert Ellis, that people need specific assignments, or 'homework'. My own perspective on psychotherapy and my interest in personal and corporate management prompted me to write a chapter on self-organisation, both at home and at work, using the 'management by objectives' approach. Drawing on the work of many experts in the field, I show clearly how to organise yourself effectively so as to tackle the challenges at hand. These challenges may be as varied as undertaking a degree or managing an anxiety attack before speaking in public.

The other action chapter in the book is on assertiveness training. This movement, which has been gaining ground for a number of years, has much to offer, not only to people with emotional problems but to all who wish to learn how to express their needs and feelings in an appropriate way. The natural tendency of systems is towards increased lack of communication or chaos, and the last two chapters are designed to overcome those periods of chaos that occur at various times, often in conjunction with emotional disturbance. The book is designed as an instructional manual that people can refer to regularly to challenge and dispute their irrational beliefs, and to remind themselves that there are almost always other options than the either/or approach that is so common in day-to-day life.

Antony Kidman

Acknowledgements

I would like to thank Dr Albert Ellis and Dr Aaron Beck for their comments and the ideas that they have expressed in their publications, together with the opportunity to discuss psychotherapy with them on various occasions.

I would like to thank the staff of the Institute for Rational-Emotive Therapy in New York for their supervision and assistance during my training there.

I wish to thank the following for permission to produce copyright material:

Dr Aaron T Beck, for the Anxiety Checklist on page 41 (© Aaron T Beck, MD, 1978); the Daily Record of Dysfunctional Thoughts appearing on pages 28–29 (© Aaron T Beck, MD, 1977). Further information about them and permission to use and reproduce them may be obtained from the Center for Cognitive Therapy, Room 602, 133 South 36th Street, Philadelphia, Pennsylvania 19104, USA.

The Institute for Rational-Emotive Therapy, New York, for the RET Self-Help Form on pages 118–21. Further information about it and permission to use it may be obtained from the Institute of Rational-Emotive Therapy, 45 East 65th Street, New York, NY 10021–6593, USA.

Dr Jeffrey E Young, Department of Psychiatry, Columbia University, to use his Loneliness Scale on pages 58–62, and Dr E Gambrill, to use the Gambrill and Richey Assertion Inventory, which first appeared in the *Journal of Behaviour Therapy*, Volume 6, pages 550–561 in 1975, and which appears on pages 85–87.

Antony Kidman

CHAPTER 1
Introduction

How to use this book

How To Change Your Life is a self-help manual, designed to show you how to deal with events going on in the world around you, how to achieve your goals and, most importantly, how to deal with yourself and self-defeating behaviour. It covers different topics from my first book, *Tactics for Changing Your Life* (Kogan Page, 1989), and can be used by itself or along with this book.

Read the Introduction and skim through the book, marking in the Contents the chapters or sections that interest you most, then go to the most relevant chapter and read it right through. Make a copy of the questionnaire or assessment form and fill it in. Use a blank sheet of paper to write out some plan you will follow to work on the problem at hand. Then go to the next section and follow the same procedure. I suggest that everyone read Chapter 5, on Self-organisation, and copy the forms because, above all else, they will help you to tackle your problems in a systematic fashion. Re-read and mark relevant sections or phrases. Keep the book handy so you can refer to it when you need to. Cut out the rational responses on pages 122–3 and put them on your noticeboard, bathroom mirror or in your wallet so that you are regularly reminded of them.

I have drawn heavily on the work of Dr Albert Ellis, founder of Rational-Emotive Therapy, and Dr Aaron Beck, who calls his aproach Cognitive Therapy. They argue that there is a fundamental relationship between the external world (A) which impinges on a person's belief system or thinking patterns (B) and that those thoughts then generate feelings (C) and behaviour patterns.

B. Thoughts

You interpret the events with a series of thoughts that continually flow through your mind. This is called your 'self talk'

A. Environment

A series of positive, neutral and negative events

C. Mood

Your feelings are created by your thoughts. All experiences must be processed through your brain and given a conscious meaning before you experience an emotional response

The first step to deal with what you perceive to be a problem, or even a crisis, is to change your negative feeling of anxiety or hostility or whatever into the more appropriate one of concern or annoyance. This is done by working on your belief system (B) so that you are then in a suitable frame of mind to tackle the problems of the external world and the goals you have set. It is then possible to turn crises into challenges and to approach them in a sensible way.

The chapters Coping With Anxiety and Overcoming Loneliness deal with common but highly disturbing feelings that beset all of us from time to time and some of us chronically. Feelings can be worked on and changed by disputing and challenging any negative thoughts, but they require persistent effort. There is *no* magic solution but the rewards of persistence are well worthwhile.

The chapters Assertiveness Training and Self-organisation describe how you can work on the external world and achieve the goals you have set for yourself by planning and taking action.

Challenge your irrational thinking

Albert Ellis asserts that almost all emotional disturbance is due to irrational thinking, and a list of his ten common irrational ideas is given below.

List of common irrational ideas

1. I must be loved or approved of by every significant person in my life.
2. I must be competent, adequate and achieving in all respects if I am to consider myself worthwhile.
3. When people act unfairly or badly, I blame them and they should be severely punished.
4. It is terrible and catastrophic when things are not the way I would very much like them to be.
5. Human unhappiness is caused by external events and people have little or no ability to control their sorrows and disturbances.
6. I must feel anxious if something is or may be dangerous or fearsome and keep dwelling on the possibility of its occurrence.
7. It is easier to avoid than to face certain difficulties in life with responsibility.
8. Everyone should be dependent upon others and I need someone stronger than myself on whom I can rely.
9. I should become quite upset over other people's problems and disturbances.
10. The world should provide me with what I need and when it doesn't, it's a terrible place and I can't stand it.

(A number of rational coping statements are shown on pages 122–3 and can be cut out and placed in your wallet or on your notice board as reminders to dispute your irrational self-talk.)

This list can be reduced to two *demands*:

1. The world should be a perfect place and give me everything I want for very little effort and, when it doesn't, I cannot stand it.
2. People, including myself, should behave in certain ways and, when we don't, we deserve to be punished severely.

The key word here is *'should'* and the so-called 'tyranny of the shoulds' – a phrase first used by psychiatrist Karen Horney – operates extensively in human thinking and behaviour. A rational statement would be:

I would *prefer* the world to be a perfect place and that people, including myself, behave as I wish, but I will accept that we have not yet nor are ever likely to achieve Utopia. Things will often not be as I want; thus I am not going to get exceptionally angry, depressed or guilty. However, being human, I will become appropriately annoyed, sad or concerned. I can do that by challenging my thinking and internal self-dialogue.

The Dysfunctional Thoughts Schedule shown on page 28 or the RET Self-Help Form on page 118 can be used, for example, to strengthen this rational self-talk. The technique is also called self-instructional training.

Anxiety

We are told that this is the age of anxiety and Chapter 2, devoted to this subject, was written first. I have tried to show people how to manage and reduce the anxiety that immobilises and prevents them from achieving their goals. I describe the symptoms and a number of cognitive behavioural methods to reduce those unpleasant and frequently overwhelming feelings. Many who suffer from anxiety, whether due to a specific situation or the generalised free-floating type, fear their feelings so much that their anxiety about their anxiety becomes an ever-worsening cycle. Dysfunctional Thought Forms and an assessment questionnaire are included.

Loneliness

Loneliness is another common unpleasant feeling and is dealt with in Chapter 3. Many lonely people are also anxious, so the techniques in Chapter 2 can also be used. They are often depressed and, in my previous book, *Tactics for Changing Your Life*, I deal with this.

The objective is to turn feelings of loneliness into solitude and then to work on developing friendships and intimate relationships. Before you do anything to try to change the outside world, it is essential to work on mentally re-evaluating events in the world and thus change your attitude to it.

Taking action

Besides challenging your thinking, it is necessary to start working on objectives and meeting challenges with action. You may learn to become less upset about events in your life, but you have very little chance of changing what can be changed if you do not take action. The chapters on Assertiveness Training and Self-organisation show you how to take action. Assertive individuals express their feelings and needs and know how to deal with people at home and at work in a non-aggressive way. These techniques can be learnt by anyone who is willing to absorb them and practise them.

Almost all of us in the business world and in family life would like to be more effectively organised. I have spoken to many people about self- and time management. Short- and long-term plans are the key to self-organisation. Writing them out is described in detail so that they can be regularly reviewed, revised and followed. These techniques will enable students to tackle big assignments, working people to achieve goals both at the office and at home, and they enable everyone to attain qualifications and acquire skills. However, it requires persistent effort directed against our natural tendencies to give up, throw up our hands in despair and say, 'It's too hard.'

Low frustration tolerance

Most of us start out with a low level of frustration tolerance because of our culture, the media, the way we were indulged by parents and relatives and the general unrealistic expectations that good things should happen to us with the minimum of effort on our part. We *should* be able to attain high marks in exams, we *should* be able to get a top paying job and become the boss within a short time, we *should* have a fine home and a good relationship, we *should* have a smart car.

Some people are lucky and there is no law in the universe that says there shall be justice and fairness to all. Some people inherit wealth, some win a lottery or make a killing on the stock market. The majority, however, do not. They work hard for their success and even then it is not guaranteed. In general *there is no gain without pain*. This means working to combat your natural tendencies to say, 'I'll never achieve this', 'It's not fair that . . .' and 'I can't stand it.'

I say to patients and to myself as often as I can, 'Where is it written that you shouldn't have to put up with frustration and discomfort in your life at some time?' Some people with severe physical handicaps put up with severe frustration for much of their lives. However, many of them, by determination and effort, achieve their goals despite their handicap.

There are others with no physical handicaps who have 'biological handicaps' (depression, anxiety) who reinforce these tendencies by telling themselves they cannot put up with discomfort. 'If others can, you can' is a good challenging statement that will help to raise your frustration tolerance.

I suggest strongly to people that they seek out and stay with discomforting situations in order to (a) raise their tolerance levels and (b) learn to appreciate the pleasant experiences in their lives. I do not mean that you should continuously seek out *unpleasant* experiences but rather plan to have some enjoyable goal at the end, such as attaining a degree, playing the piano, speaking a foreign language, jogging steadily for 40 minutes, and enjoy the rewards and pleasures of your achievement. I urge you to accept short- to medium-term frustration in order to achieve rewarding and pleasurable longer-term goals.

I believe healthy people accept responsibility for their actions and that they plan for the future as well as enjoying their lives now. We did not ask to be born but we *can* choose to make our lives more enjoyable.

References

A T Beck, *Cognitive Therapy and Emotional Disorders*, International Universities Press, New York (1976)

A Ellis, *Reason and Emotion in Psychotherapy*, Citadel, USA (1985)

S I Hayakawa, *Language in Thought and Action*, Harcourt Brace Jovanovich, 4th Ed (1978)

CHAPTER 2
Coping With Anxiety

What is anxiety?

Anxiety is a universal, human experience that is characterised by fearful anticipation of a possible unpleasant event. It is important to distinguish between anxiety and fear because they are often used interchangeably. Fear is the assessment of danger; anxiety is the unpleasant feelings and symptoms evoked when fear is stimulated. A person suffering from anxiety experiences an unpleasant emotional state characterised by tension, nervousness, heart palpitations, tremor, nausea, dizziness, immobility, inability to think clearly and, on some occasions, inability even to speak; other symptoms may include backache, headache and diarrhoea. All of us have felt intensely anxious at times and it is estimated that about 5 per cent of the population suffer from chronic anxiety, with women outnumbering men two to one.

Professor Aaron Beck claims that people with anxiety disorders have unrealistic fears because they wrongly assess the danger associated with a particular situation. These erroneous assessments are usually due to one or more of the following:

1. Overestimating the chance of a dangerous event, eg 'The bus in which I am being driven is likely to crash.'
2. Overestimating the severity of the feared event, eg 'If I lose my job I will be finished and I can't see anything else for me.'
3. Underestimating how you'll cope (what you can do to help yourself).
4. Underestimating rescue factors (what other people can do to help you).

Anxiety is a problem when it occurs in the absence of any real danger or when it continues long after the stress is over. It is normal and appropriate to be keyed up (or anxious) before a football game or to feel some anxiety before an exam because this often makes us perform at our best, as the body systems speed up and this can be an advantage. However, if these sensations occur when you do not have to take action, it feels unpleasant. Then you will notice only the disadvantages (all the uncomfortable aspects of these bodily changes). This is when anxiety begins to interfere with everyday life and it becomes necessary to learn how to control it.

Generalised or 'free-floating' anxiety

Many people become anxious when spontaneous, negative self-talk starts and distorts their perception of reality. Vague thoughts occur that danger is lurking, that you should not be having a good time because eventually you will suffer for it, or that others think badly of you and want to do you harm. These thoughts and feelings can produce 'free-floating' anxiety, which is self-defeating. Such people worry about events that have occurred in the past or that may happen in the future. *Worrying* about these events will affect *you*, not the events themselves. It is *appropriate* to be concerned about things that have happened or may happen, and to take appropriate action; it is *inappropriate* to be so concerned that your ability to function and deal with these events is impaired.

For example, on Friday afternoon your superior (whom you do not like) asks you to see him first thing Monday morning without saying what it is about. For some people this would make for a terrible weekend: the theatre party on Saturday night and the barbecue that had been planned for Sunday would not be enjoyed because of such thoughts as:

- 'Am I going to be fired?' 'Has my performance been poor of late?'
- 'Am I going to be transferred?'
- 'I can't stand not knowing what it's all about.'

Others would use a *rational response* to challenge these irrational thoughts, such as:

- 'There may be some particular issues he wants to discuss and the worry and spoiling of my weekend will not help me at all.'
- 'I know my performance has been satisfactory. My worrying about the discussion on Monday morning is not going to help. Moreover, if I present myself in a nervous, agitated state, my ability to argue my case will be affected.'
- 'I am certainly concerned about what he will say, but I refuse to let myself be inappropriately upset by the thought of it.'

Panic disorder

How many of us at some time have been suddenly overcome with intense apprehension? Physically, we feel jumpy; cognitively, we expect that something bad is going to happen. Such an attack comes out of nowhere – no specific object or event sets it off – and the attack gradually subsides. However, some people have frequent severe attacks. These people suffer from panic disorder.

Emotionally, the person is overwhelmed with intense apprehension, dread or terror. Physically, symptoms appear – rapid heart beat, muscle tension, perspiration, trembling. Cognitively, the person thinks he may die, go mad or lose control of himself. There is no definitive data on the incidence of panic attacks, although they are quite common. Clinical experience, however, indicates that they occur more frequently in women than in men and that they can be clearly distinguished from a phobia.

Phobia

A phobia is a persistent anxiety reaction that is grossly out of proportion to the stimulus and the reality of the danger. There are a variety of things or activities in the world that produce inordinate and irrational fear in many people, including flying, snakes, spiders, mice, water, having to talk to strangers, lifts, crowded places. The point is that some relatively harmless object or activity produces these feelings. Even though there is the *possibility* of a plane crashing, or of being bitten by a spider, the *chances* of it happening are so low that the emotional response is totally out of proportion to the risk of being harmed. This type of response is a phobia.

The phobic reaction may interfere with the person's entire life. Recently, I heard of a case where a person had not left his home for more than 30 years, having been cared for by a relative. When that relative died, the person was in danger of starving to death as he would not leave that safe place to shop. This is an extreme example of agoraphobia – literally, the fear of the market-place. Such people will not leave designated safe places, such as their home, to go into the street, to shop, to use public transport. The further they are from their 'safe' haven, the more anxious they become, fearing that they will die, be attacked or lose control of themselves. Agoraphobia can severely restrict normal life and cause great emotional disturbance.

About 8 per cent of the population have mild phobias – stronger than intense fear but not severely limiting – and 0.2 per cent have severe phobias, that is, those so strong they might keep the person housebound, as in the example above. These are *prevalence rates*, that is the percentage of the population having a disorder at any given time in contrast to *incidence*, which is the rate of new cases of a disorder in a given period.

The anxiety model

The anxiety cycle shown on page 24 is an example of the ABC model of Dr Albert Ellis described in Chapter 1. The external world (A) is perceived and thoughts are generated as a result (B). Negative thoughts about some future event will then produce the feelings of anxiety in the person (C). The behaviour patterns following the anxiety include restlessness, insomnia, inability to work and/or to relate to others. It is important to note in the model that the feelings and the unpleasant bodily sensations generated by the thoughts become the source of *more* negative thoughts and thus an ever-worsening cycle is set up.

Anxiety cycle

(A) EXTERNAL EVENTS

(B) NEGATIVE THOUGHTS

(C) FEELING OF ANXIETY

(Unpleasant bodily sensations)

Events cause negative thoughts, or automatic negative thoughts arise spontaneously. This triggers feelings of anxiety and unpleasant bodily sensations. This in turn leads to more negative thoughts and increased feelings of anxiety. Thus an ever worsening cycle is generated.

Alternatively, a bodily sensation, quickening heartbeat or slight pain in the chest or stomach is misinterpreted by the mind and triggers an escalating cycle of anxiety.

'Why am I anxious and what can I do about it?'

These are the questions that the people who suffer from anxiety ask me again and again. They also ask:

- 'Are there some special drugs I can take that would solve the problem?'
- 'Should I give up trying for a while and take a long rest?'
- 'There must be somebody who can cure me. Who can I go to see?'

Let me try to answer these questions in the following way. People have anxiety problems because they may have a hereditary predisposition to over-react more than other people or they may have learnt to react to problems in a certain way over many years. This does not mean that they cannot learn how to manage their anxiety. Medication can provide some temporary relief but before long the tablets become less and less effective so that more need to be taken to achieve the same effect. If the problem is related to thoughts and feelings, *that* is where the solution lies. Nobody can 'cure' anxiety as it is a normal part of everyday life. However, you can work on the problem and, with professional help in some cases, learn to reduce anxiety. I describe ways to do that in the following sections.

Techniques for managing anxiety

Challenging irrational thoughts

Dr Albert Ellis, founder of Rational-Emotive Therapy, was one of the first of the modern cognitive-behavioural psychologists to advocate disputing irrational thinking and to promote this as a tool in psychotherapy. His book, *Reason and Emotion in Psychotherapy*, lists 11 *irrational beliefs* which cause problems. These include:

1. If something is or may be dangerous or fearsome one should be terribly concerned about it and should keep dwelling on the possibility of it occurring.
2. Human unhappiness is externally caused and people have little or no ability to control their sorrows or problems.
3. It is easier to avoid than to face certain of life's difficulties and responsibilities.

The thoughts that are associated with these and other irrational ideas produce anxiety and anxious behaviour. For example, you are worrying about the possibility of losing your job owing to circumstances beyond your control; the economy is bad and the company is making people redundant. The sequence of thinking → feelings → behaviour needs to be broken and the fundamental technique alluded to earlier is that of *self-talk*.

Self-talk is literally answering your internal critic and disputing negative thoughts when they enter your head. Let us assume that you may be made redundant because of an economic downturn. Typical negative thoughts may be:

- 'I am a failure if I lose my job.'
- 'How am I going to survive if I lose this job?'
- 'What will my friends think if I am out of work?'

Countering, anxiety-reducing self-talk would be:

- 'I may fail to hold this job but I myself am not a failure.' 'It is not the worst thing that can happen to me and I can stand it!'
- 'Thousands of others have survived periods of unemployment and if it is forced on me, I will look for another job and try to develop new skills.'
- 'So what if they think badly of me. I would like them to approve of me but I cannot demand their approval."

Ellis uses the word *'catastrophising'* to describe the great deal of anxiety generated by our tendency to think of the worst possible outcome when there are almost always other options.

A very useful way to 'decatastrophise' is to insert the phrase, 'So what if ...' before the thought; 'So what if I get blown up by my boss! I can handle that, I have done so before. I will be more cooperative and try to work more effectively or I will work out a definite plan to get a new job.'

Dr Beck's cognitive therapy approach is similar and following are two of his special Daily Record of Dysfunctional Thoughts forms. One is filled in as an example, the other is blank so that you can use it to write down your automatic negative thoughts and feelings and the rational countering statements.

The examples show that writing down negative thoughts and feelings and then disputing them with rational statements can significantly reduce your anxiety level. There is also a blank RET self-help form which serves the same purpose.

I believe this is one of the most effective methods of dealing with anxiety, ie to recognise the role of automatic negative thoughts and the fact that we *generally magnify the possibility of disaster*. You can dispute your thinking and thus break the cycle that intensifies the unpleasant feelings.

Thought stopping

This is a simple technique that many people find useful when they have a worrying thought that is making them anxious. You sit back, relax and close your eyes, put your hands on your knees and let the thought that has been bothering you deliberately come into your mind. For example, 'The future is hopeless.' As soon as the thought comes to mind, say, 'Stop', loudly, and then open your eyes. If the thought is still with you, repeat the procedure and say it again. I suggest you repeat this at least ten times. Thought stopping generally becomes more effective with practice and it is better to say 'Stop' a hundred times than to have the thought you want to eliminate persist. Keeping the thought doesn't get you anywhere, it just makes you feel upset. If you apply this thought stopping procedure constantly, you will notice that, gradually, the thought will occur less and less until it goes away completely.

Relaxation

This is another wisely used technique to help manage anxiety. It has been used for hundreds of years by all sorts of people in conjunction with meditation. Edmund Jacobsen of Chicago introduced progressive muscle relaxation, but recently the work of Herbert Benson of the Harvard Medical School and Arnold Lazarus of Rutgers University has been widely publicised and I would like to draw on some of their findings. Try this:

1. Sit quietly in a comfortable position, with legs uncrossed and your feet flat on the floor. Put your hands on your thighs and try to relax.
2. Close your eyes.
3. Tighten and relax the muscles of your body in sequence, beginning with your feet. When you tense a muscle, notice where it is particularly tense, then notice how it feels when you relax it.

Daily Record of Dysfunctional Thoughts Form

Date	Situation Describe: 1. Actual event leading to unpleasant emotion, or 2. Stream of thoughts, daydream, or recollection, leading to unpleasant emotion.	Emotions(s) 1. Specify sad; anxious; angry etc. 2. Rate degree of emotion, 1–100 per cent.	Automatic thought(s) 1. Write automatic thought(s) that precede emotion(s). 2. Rate belief in automatic thought(s), 0–100 per cent.
9/9	Was thinking of all the things I want to get done over the weekend.	1. Anxious 2. 40%	1. I'll never get all this done. It's too much for me. 2. 100%
9/11	Made a mistake ordering supplies.	1. Anxious 2. 60%	1. Pictured my boss yelling at me. 2. 100%
21/11	At a function with strangers, felt they were watching me.	1. Anxious 2. 70%	1. People are looking at me. I must be doing something wrong; perhaps I said something stupid. 2. 90%
3/12	Felt my heart start to beat fast as I came into a crowded supermarket.	1. Anxious 2. 90%	1. I am going to have an attack of something and die or go mad. 2. 100%

Rational response 1. Write rational response to automatic thought(s). 2. Rate belief in rational response, 0–100 per cent.	Outcome 1. Re-rate belief in automatic thought(s), 1–100 per cent. 2. Specify and rate subsequent emotions, 0–100 per cent.
1. I've done more than this before, and there is no law that says I have to get it done. 2. 90%	1. 25% 2. Anxious 20%
1. There is no evidence my boss will be angry, and even if he is I don't have to be upset. 2. 100%	1. 5% 2. Anxious 10%
1. I am standing around like anyone else, no one is pointing at me. So people do that from time to time. 2. 95%	1. 10% 2. Anxious 10%
1. Nothing is going to happen to me here. People often get strange sensations. I will start breathing slowly. 2. 80%	1. 40% 2. Anxious 40%

Daily Record of Dysfunctional Thoughts Form

Date	Situation Describe: 1. Actual event leading to unpleasant emotion, or 2. Stream of thoughts, daydream, or recollection, leading to unpleasant emotion.	Emotions(s) 1. Specify sad; anxious; angry etc. 2. Rate degree of emotion, 1–100 per cent.	Automatic thought(s) 1. Write automatic thought(s) that precede emotion(s). 2. Rate belief in automatic thought(s), 0–100 per cent.

How to fill in the form:

When you experience an unpleasant emotion, note the situation that seemed to stimulate the emotion. (If the emotion occurred while you were thinking, daydreaming, etc, please note this.) Then note the automatic thought associated with the emotion. Record the degree to which you believe this thought: 0% = not at all; 100% = completely. In rating degree of emotion: 1 = a trace; 100 = the most intense possible.

Rational response	**Outcome**
1. Write rational response to automatic thought(s). 2. Rate belief in rational response, 0–100 per cent.	1. Re-rate belief in automatic thought(s), 1–100 per cent. 2. Specify and rate subsequent emotions, 0–100 per cent.

The sequence then is to: tense; scan; relax and enjoy the pleasant feeling.

Next, progress to the muscles in your legs, thighs, buttocks, stomach, chest, arms, hands, neck and face.

Now try to relax your whole body and notice any part that is still tense and try to relax it.

4. Become aware of your breathing. As you breathe out, say the word 'relax' silently to yourself, ie breathe in, breathe out, then say 'relax'. Breathe easily and naturally.

5. In your mind's eye, imagine a pleasant scene – something from the past which was particularly enjoyable or some future event you are looking forward to. For example, imagine yourself in a beautiful forest, you are walking with a friend, the day is sunny and warm, you can hear the sounds of birds and the air is clean and fresh. The sun is coming through the trees and all your worries and concerns have been left behind. There is nothing that concerns you now ....

   You could use a beach scene instead or whatever pleases you. Remember, imagery is a very important tool in reducing anxiety and it *improves with practice*.

6. Continue this imagery and breathing for 10 to 20 minutes. You may open your eyes to check the time, but do not use an alarm. When you have finished, sit quietly for a few minutes, first with your eyes closed, then with your eyes open.

Do not worry about whether you are successful in achieving deep, mental relaxation; maintain a passive attitude and allow relaxation to occur at its own pace. When distracting thoughts occur, let them pass through your mind, and work on your imagery. With practice a relaxed response should come with little effort. Try the technique once or twice daily, but not within two hours of any meal as the digestive processes seem to interfere with the relaxation response.

You can practise mini-relaxation sessions at other times, such as when you are sitting in a waiting room, on a bus or when about to be interviewed for a new job. You can close your eyes, concentrate on your breathing and use imagery even if it's only for 30 seconds or a minute. This will help to calm you and prepare you for what you are about to do.

I suggest that if you suffer from frequent anxiety you should try to relax when you sit. Don't sit on the edge of your chair, don't hunch your shoulders, don't clench your fists. In other words, try to adopt a relaxed posture. Being tense can be very tiring. Allow your body to rest comfortably, even when performing tasks. For example, try to relax when eating meals, waiting in a queue or driving your car.

Exercise

The techniques already mentioned use thinking and imagination to reduce anxiety. I now want to discuss exercise and its role in changing feelings and controlling anxiety.

Any activity that increases heart rate and blood flow throughout the body is classified as aerobic exercise. Good examples of this are jogging, fast walking, swimming, cycling and tennis. All of these can be done readily without going to special classes. Fast walking in particular is one of the easiest and it does not require any special clothing or equipment.

Dr Kenneth Cooper, who has written many books on aerobic exercise, recommends that it be performed at least three times a week for a minimum of 30 minutes to achieve and maintain an adequate level of aerobic fitness. According to Dr Cooper, people who achieve and maintain this level are able to carry out their daily tasks more effectively, get less fatigued than if they were not fit and enjoy an increased sense of well-being. Before starting such an exercise routine, have a medical check-up. If you have not exercised for some time or you are over 30, this is essential.

In dealing with anxiety, however, we are not so much concerned with aerobic fitness but rather the use of vigorous exercise to help bring about changes in feelings. I tell people that, when anxiety starts to mount, vigorous activity can help. The feelings of anxiety will frequently reduce during or at the end of the activity. Imagery can be used during the process and the feeling of well-being that follows a fast walk or workout can be reinforced by a relaxation session, using the technique described.

I recommend Dr Cooper's book *New Aerobics* and suggest that an aerobic fitness programme could be taken up as a preventive measure for chronic anxiety.

Distraction

Included in this general technique are two methods already described – imagery and physical exercise. They help to replace upsetting thoughts with more appropriate ones. Other activities that can distract and turn off the thoughts that keep bombarding the mind are:

- Concentrating on what is happening around you. For example, you could listen to someone else's conversation or count how many different blue things you can see. Choose something that holds your attention. When distracting yourself it helps to adopt a specific task, like guessing what jobs people do or deciding what you would buy in each shop window you pass.
- Mental activity, which includes such things as doing mental arithmetic, reciting a poem to yourself, doing a crossword puzzle or pushing yourself to read an article or book, can also distract you.

By using one of these activities, many people feel better because they have stopped paying attention to their symptoms, which will then often disappear of their own accord.

Systematic desensitisation

This is a core procedure of behaviour therapy developed by Dr Joseph Wolpe. It involves three phases:

1. Put yourself into a relaxed state (as described previously on page 27).
2. Imagine a sequence of situations of progressively increasing intensity centred around the anxiety-provoking event or thing. Dwell on each scene for several minutes and experience the anxiety generated by each.
3. Relax again and imagine each scene again in the same

BASICALLY, IMAGINE YOURSELF IN A POTENTIALLY ANXIOUS SCENE BUT BEING ABLE TO DO SOMETHING TO THWART THE ANXIETY.

sequence, but this time imagine yourself coping with the situation. The feelings of anxiety will recede.

An example of a sequence of situations using this technique could be a woman who is fearful of making contact with strangers. She sits in a chair and imagines the following schenes:

1. People in a bus queue chatting to one another, complaining about waiting. She joins in the general complaints.
2. She is sitting at a table having lunch when two other people sit down at her table. A conversation about the weather and the quality of the food ensues. She contributes to this conversation.
3. Sitting in a doctor's waiting room, she initiates a conversation with the person sitting next to her.
4. She enters a crowded room at a party and starts to chat with some people she does not know.
5. She phones someone she has met only once and suggests that they go out together.

Dr Wolpe claims considerable success with this technique and many people I have worked with find it helpful.

'In vivo' techniques

Another technique that is very effective in overcoming anxiety is to directly confront the person or circumstance as often as you can. This often leads to the realisation that the situation was not so bad after all and the dire predictions you made about the outcome were misplaced.

A recent case in my experience is that of a man with severe anxiety about public speaking. Being a senior executive it was often necessary for him to speak in public. His anxiety had reached such heights that sometimes he was physically sick before speaking. He was given an assignment over the next two weeks to speak six times at small gatherings within his organisation. He did so and reported that, despite feeling extremely anxious at the first meeting, he managed it and by the sixth meeting his anxiety levels were considerably reduced.

Another example is that of a lonely widower who wished to

make contact with women but was extremely anxious about being rejected by them. His assignment was to engage women in polite conversation so that there was the opportunity for him to be rejected by them at least ten times in a week. This was to allow him to become desensitised to rejection, which occurs frequently in interpersonal transactions, and to learn that rejection is an integral part of establishing new friendships. He completed this assignment although he had terrible feelings while doing it. Six women had rebuffed him but he had interesting conversations with the other four. One had even agreed to meet him again for lunch. He felt that he had learnt a lot from this exercise and he was now willing to take risks in establishing friendships, because rejection was not as bad as he had imagined.

A technique described by Albert Ellis to overcome anxiety about feelings of disapproval from others is to undertake 'shame attacking' behaviour. A typical assignment is to go up to individuals or groups of people in the street and simply tell them the time of day. This may seem unusual and prompts a variety of reactions from people, including disapproval and/or puzzled looks. After doing this on several occasions the anxiety about what people will think is lessened. These and other 'shame attacking' assignments enable individuals with a dire need for approval to do things that they have been wanting to do to enjoy their lives more.

Graded practice

It is best to tackle anxiety provoking situations in a systematic fashion, working up gradually as follows:

1. Make a list of the situations that make you anxious and that you avoid, using the Target List on page 37.
2. Arrange these in the order of how difficult it is for you to face them.
3. Select the easiest situation on your list as your first target, plan how to handle it, then start doing it.
4. Make yourself do the thing many times and, sooner or later, it will become easier.
5. Move to the next item on your list.

Target List

How to fill in your target list

1. Make a list of all those situations that you avoid or make you anxious.
2. Arrange these in order of difficulty.
3. Express each one in clear terms, and write them in the space provided below.

Target

1. ....

....

2. ....

....

3. ....

....

4. ....

....

5. ....

....

6. ....

....

7. ....

....

8. ....

(Please use another sheet of paper if you need more room.)

Planning

I argue very strongly that it is in people's interest to reduce stress in their lives by practising time management. This means *preparing a written list of objectives* on a daily, weekly, monthly, even yearly basis. In Chapter 5, Self-organisation, I give details of these techniques.

By planning you can approach living with a *problem-solving attitude* rather than with an anxiety-provoking 'not another crisis' attitude. If you are willing to schedule your activities in advance and, most importantly, assign priorities to them, you can decide what short- and long-term goals are important to you. There may be many things you are doing that you do not really *need* to do, and only by planning your activities in advance can you decide whether they are important or not. Often urgent demands, such as someone insisting that you come and help at a school fête or that you ring back someone within the next hour, may not be important for you at all. If so, don't do them.

Systematic preparation of a 'To do today' list, together with scheduled periods of leisure or simply doing nothing, is most important for all of us. Ask yourself, 'What are some of the things I really like doing?' Going to films, singing around a piano, walking at dusk, riding horses?' Schedule some of these pleasurable activities into your life – see the chapter Risk Taking in my book *Tactics for Changing Your Life* (Kogan Page). The rushing around that we see in our own lives and those of others is not necessary. The 'hurry syndrome', as I call it, is often the result of the anxious feelings that occur within us.

Remember AWARE

When you suddenly become anxious or panic-stricken because of something that has happened, it is difficult to think clearly. It is even more difficult to act appropriately and, for this reason, you should learn beforehand what course of action to take. The key to switching off an anxiety state is to accept it fully; remaining in the present and accepting your anxiety will help it to disappear. Use the five-step AWARE strategy to eliminate anxiety:

1. **A**gree to receive your anxiety.
   Say to yourself, 'I'll accept and deal with this!' Your feelings of dread at the thought of it coming over you again will only worsen by resisting. Instead, flow with it. Don't make *it* responsible for how *you* think, feel and act.
2. **W**atch your anxiety.
   Think of yourself outside your body as an independent observer watching what is happening. Note how your anxiety level rises and falls. Remember you are not your anxiety. The more you can separate yourself from the experience the more you can watch it.
3. **A**ct as if the anxiety is not there.
   Pretend the situation is normal. Act as if you are not anxious. Go with it. Slow down if you have to, breathe slowly and normally, but keep going. If you run from the situation your anxiety will go down for the moment but your thoughts about the situation in the future will bring it back again, perhaps to an even higher level.
4. **R**epeat the steps:
   (a) Accept your anxiety.
   (b) Watch your anxiety.
   (c) Act as if the anxiety is not there.
   Flow with the anxiety until it subsides to a comfortable level, which it will do if you continue to accept, agree, watch and act on it. Just keep repeating these steps.
5. **E**xpect the best!
   What you worry about most rarely happens. Don't be distressed the next time you experience anxiety; instead, surprise yourself with your ability to handle it. As long as you live there will be some anxiety in your life. To accept this fact puts you in a better position to cope with anxiety when it next occurs.

As part of the AWARE strategy, monitor each anxiety state by keeping a diary. Jot down a few notes and rate your anxiety on a 0-100 scale. This helps you to separate yourself from your anxiety – to become an independent observer.

Measuring anxiety

Following is the Beck Anxiety Checklist. It lists a number of symptoms and the frequency with which they occur. Make as many photocopies as you want for your own use.

I suggest you circle the items as instructed and record the date. After using one or more of the techniques for managing anxiety for about two weeks, complete a second anxiety checklist to compare with the first.

Continue to use this form to monitor your progress at two-weekly intervals.

Medication

Drug treatment (pharmacotherapy) for anxiety is frequently used by medical practitioners and is appropriate in certain circumstances. However, there is a tendency to offer anti-anxiety drugs as the main, and for many the only, treatment. The cognitive/behavioural techniques I have described earlier are educational and require understanding by the therapist and the patient. The therapist monitors the treatment and provides feedback to the patient as treatment progresses.

The drugs that are used to treat anxiety can be divided into four groups and it is important that people know how they act and what to expect from them. The groups are:

1. Major tranquillisers
2. Minor tranquillisers
3. Barbiturates
4. Beta-blockers

Major tranquillisers

This group includes drugs such as chlorpromazine (Largactil), thioradazine (Melleril) and haloperidol (Serenace). What makes this group of drugs different from other anti-anxiety drugs is that they are also used to treat major psychiatric problems such as schizophrenia and severe emotional disorders. However, they may be prescribed for anxiety and tension.

Beck Anxiety Checklist

Name .... Date ....

How to fill in your inventory
Below is a list of common symptoms of anxiety. Please read each item in the list carefully. Indicate *how much* you have been bothered by each symptom during the PAST WEEK, INCLUDING TODAY, by circling the corresponding number in the column to each symptom.

	Not at all	Mildly It did not bother me much	Moderately It was very unpleasant but I could stand it	Severely I could barely stand it
1. Numbness or tingling	0	1	2	3
2. Feeling hot	0	1	2	3
3. Wobbliness in legs	0	1	2	3
4. Inability to relax	0	1	2	3
5. Fear of the worst happening	0	1	2	3
6. Dizziness or lightheadedness	0	1	2	3
7. Heart pounding or racing	0	1	2	3
8. Unsteadiness	0	1	2	3
9. Terror	0	1	2	3
10. Nervousness	0	1	2	3
11. Feeling of choking	0	1	2	3
12. Hands trembling	0	1	2	3
13. Shakiness	0	1	2	3
14. Fear of losing control	0	1	2	3
15. Difficulty in breathing	0	1	2	3
16. Fear of dying	0	1	2	3
17. Apprehension	0	1	2	3
18. Indigestion or discomfort in abdomen	0	1	2	3
19. Faintness	0	1	2	3
20. Face flushing	0	1	2	3
21. Sweating (not due to heat)	0	1	2	3

To score: Add up the value you have circled for each symptom.

Undesirable effects. By taking a major tranquilliser, you may feel drowsy. However, even after very large doses of major tranquillisers it is unlikely that you will go into a deep sleep or coma. They rarely cause addiction, therefore withdrawal symptoms are not common. However, neurological problems, such as shaking and uncontrolled movements of certain muscles, occur in a small proportion of patients.

Minor tranquillisers

Four out of five people taking drugs to relieve anxiety are prescribed minor tranquillisers which include the range of drugs known as benzodiazepines. These include diazepam (Valium), chlordiazepoxide (Librium) and nitrazepam (Mogadon). At higher doses these drugs can be used as hypnotics or sleeping pills; at lower doses they act as anti-anxiety agents. They can reduce acute anxiety when given intravenously.

Undesirable effects. They may make you feel drowsy. They also relax the muscles, which may make some people feel a little wobbly in the legs. They may also affect your memory, making you slightly absent-minded. They have a good margin for safety and overdose problems are rare. However, large doses of these drugs over a long period can lead to staggering movements, slurred speech and double vision, especially in the elderly. Many people who take benzodiazepines for long periods can become dependent upon them. Studies suggest that after prolonged treatment about 45 per cent of users experience moderate withdrawal symptoms.

Barbiturates

These drugs will both relax you by day and make you sleep at night. They have the longest history in the treatment of anxiety and date back to the beginning of this century. Drugs in this group include amobarbital (Amytal), sodium amobarbital (Sodium Amytal), meprobamate (Equanil; Mepron), sodium secobarbital (Seconal). However, they have been largely replaced by the much safer benzodiazepines.

Undesirable effects. The use of these drugs has been increasingly restricted because of their toxicity following overdose. They can produce unexpected excitement in the elderly. They also affect the action of the liver. By increasing the rate at which other drugs are used by the liver, they may interfere with other treatment the patient may be having. For example, a person may be on a drug to reduce blood clotting, and if barbiturates are taken for anxiety this can change the effectiveness of the blood-clotting drug and cause serious problems.

Beta-blockers

These drugs have aroused interest recently as they relieve two of the common symptoms of anxiety – palpitations and shakiness. They are mainly used for treating high blood pressure. They are called beta-blockers because of their biochemical action which results in a slower heart rate and thus lowered blood pressure. If the main symptoms of a person's anxiety are rapid heartbeat and shakiness, beta-blockers may be helpful. One advantage is the low risk of dependency. Drugs such as propranolol (Inderal), metropolol (Betaloc; Lopresor) are in this group.

Undesirable effects. Because they suppress many of the stimulating effects of adrenalin (a hormone that increases heart and pulse rate, and dilates air passages), beta-blockers may cause faintness and wheezing, particularly in asthma sufferers.

Drug treatment can be appropriate for anxiety, especially to overcome extreme anxiety in some people, but for long-term results, the person's perceptions and thought patterns need to be tackled. Drugs can be helpful to get people into a frame of mind to think about their 'thinking' and to listen to and act on the advice of a professional therapist.

Alcohol, nicotine and other drugs

There is no doubt that people smoke and drink to relieve anxiety and it is often appropriate to have a glass of beer or wine or a nip of spirits to ease tension and to make people feel comfortable when they are anxious. However, the problems of becoming

Summary of drugs and their effects

Class of compound	Generic name	Trade name	Side effects
Major tranquillisers	Chlorpromazine Thioradazine Haloperidol	Largactil Melleril Serenace	Drowsiness, neurological problems in small number of people. Not addictive.
Minor tranquillisers – Benzodiazepines	Diazepam Chlordiazepoxide Nitrazepam	Valium Librium Mogadon	Drowsiness. Some people get addicted over long periods.
Barbiturates	Amobarbital Sodium amobarbital Meprobamate Sodium secobarbital	Amytal Sodium amytal Equanil, Mepron Seconal	Drowsiness. An overdose can be very serious.
Beta-blockers	Propranolol Metoprolol	Inderal Lopresor	Slower pulse rate. Can cause wheezing in asthma sufferers.

dependent upon alcohol to reduce anxiety are well known. So if you are using alcohol to reduce your anxiety, be careful! Like all other drugs it is appropriate under certain circumstances but the tendency to become dependent makes alcoholism the biggest drug abuse problem in our society.

The person who smokes may find that a cigarette is helpful in anxiety-provoking situations. However, because of the health risks associated with this habit, it would be wiser to consider using some other method to reduce anxiety.

People use other drugs, too, such as cocaine, heroin and

marijuana to help cope with their anxiety. These have many undesirable effects, including physical and psychological addiction, that are well documented.

Conclusion

Many people wonder why they are anxiety prone. This is not vitally important to them as long as they can learn techniques to manage their anxiety. One suggestion which is worth recording is that 'normal' individuals who don't suffer from inordinate anxiety develop a tolerance for moderately frightening situations after repeated exposure to them, while the 'anxiety prone' individuals not only fail to become used to these stimuli – such as heights or flying in planes – but actually become more anxious with each exposure.

Research workers at Oxford University found that sequences of startling sounds presented to both a control and a highly anxious group of subjects produced increased perspiration in both groups. However, upon repeated exposure to the sounds, the perspiration rate of the control group decreased, while the anxious group showed sustained increased perspiration suggesting no reduction in anxiety levels. The difference in responses may be explained as follows:

The normal person is able to determine fairly rapidly that the unpleasant event is not the signal of a threat. He is able to label the sound as just that, rather than a danger signal, and his anxiety disappears. In contrast, the anxious person does not discriminate between 'safe' and 'non-safe' and continues to label the sound as a danger signal; his thinking is dominated by the concept of danger. Once something has been tagged as a danger signal, the association between it and the concept of danger becomes fixed.

Thus, it would seem that the anxiety-prone person is destined to remain a 'notice', never to become a 'seasoned veteran' whose experience of stress in the face of danger helped him to learn ways of coping with its more damaging effects.

The ideas presented here are to help 'season' vulnerable individuals and to help them to develop an immunity to their own automatic responses to danger.

Summary and reminder

When you are anxious, remember:

1. Your bodily feelings are not harmful.
2. You are not in real danger.
3. Do not run away; if you wait, the fear will pass.
4. Welcome this as a chance to practise anxiety management. Breathe slowly. Use the AWARE strategy.
5. Challenge your upsetting thoughts and record them in your diary or use one of the forms in this chapter that seems appropriate.
6. Do your relaxation exercises.
7. Distract yourself.
8. Use this list.

References

A D Kidman, *Tactics for Changing your Life*, Kogan Page (1989)

A Ellis and R A Harper, *A New Guide To Rational Living*, Wilshire, North Hollywood, California, USA (1975)

K H Cooper, *New Aerobics*, Bantam, New York (1970)

H Benson, *Relaxation Response*, Fount (1977)

H Selye, *Stress Without Distress*, Corgi, London (1987)

A A Lazarus, *In the Mind's Eye* Guildford Publications, USA (1984)

A Ellis, *Reason and Emotion in Psychotherapy*, Citadel, USA (1985)

A T Beck, G Emery and R L Greenberg, *Anxiety Disorders and Phobias: A Cognitive Perspective*, Basic Books (1985)

D L Rosenhan and M E P Seligman, *Abnormal Psychology*, W W Norton (1984)

D C Rimm and J C Masters, *Behaviour Therapy*, Academic Press (1979)

D M Clark, Cognitive Therapy for Anxiety, *Behavioural Psychotherapy* 14, pages 283–294 (1986)

J Wolpe, *The Practice of Behaviour Therapy*, Pergamon Press (1982)

CHAPTER 3
Overcoming Loneliness

Dr Bob Weiss, a sociologist at the University of Massachusetts, estimates that as many as 25 per cent of people feel extremely lonely at some time during any given month. The problem has generated a large response in the form of video matching services, computer dating, matchmaking programmes on the radio, personal introduction organisations and a variety of clubs where people can meet.

What do we mean by the term 'loneliness'? Dr Jeffrey Young of Columbia University defines loneliness as the absence, or perceived absence, of satisfying social relationships, accompanied by feelings of distress. Some people may be lonely, but not aware of it. Rather, they feel they are not enjoying relationships and the company of others and show distress in the form of anxiety, depression, insomnia and drug abuse.

Loneliness, according to another definition, is a feeling of deprivation caused by the lack of certain kinds of human contact: the feeling that something is missing; the absence of *expected* human relationships. I wish to emphasise the mental or perceptive nature of loneliness. What you think or perceive about your contact with others will determine your feelings of loneliness, and the approach I explain later on in this chapter will be not only to try to improve the nature and number of social contacts, but, more importantly, to change the perception and expectation in your mind about how you should interact with others.

People can be lonely even when they are married or living with someone. Just as *being alone* does not necessarily imply being lonely, so too being married or having friends is no certain guarantee of avoiding loneliness.

Physical separation from family and friends occurs frequently in our society. Moving to a new area, going away to another city for weeks or even months as part of your job or to study or spending an extended period in hospital are events that all affect social relationships. Separation reduces the frequency of interaction, makes the satisfactions provided by relationships less available and may raise anxiety that the relationship will be weakened by absence.

Restricted networks

People generally value a fairly rich and diverse social network that includes ties to friends, a loved partner and family. Thus a person can be lonely despite having some relationships if other important relationships are missing. For instance, a lonely housewife may be very satisfied with her marriage, but miss the companionship of female friends.

Loneliness can result not only from the absence of relationships but from dissatisfaction with the quality of existing ones. Good communication and the feeling that you are understood are very important as well as realistic expectations. I have discussed these in my book *Tactics for Changing Your Life*.

Conflict and competition inhibit self-disclosure in relationships and may contribute to feelings of loneliness as well. Unfortunately, there are many 'empty shell' marriages, relationships that provide few satisfactions to the partners who persist because of children or other barriers to divorce. The immediate environment is without laughter or fun and an atmosphere of tension or solemn gloom pervades the household. Couples do not discuss their problems or experiences with each other and communication is kept to a minimum.

Loneliness versus solitude

Loneliness, by definition, is a negative emotional state. However, *being alone* is neither a necessary nor sufficient condition for feeling lonely. As mentioned earlier, the feelings of loneliness are very much dependent upon a person's perception of what is going on in their environment.

Aloneness, or solitude, can be a very desirable state. Many people have used solitude for growth, for transcendental experiences, for creative thinking and work. Some, such as lone voyagers on boats or wanderers trekking through the wilderness, have *chosen* 'aloneness'. We all seek periods of tranquillity from time to time to re-evaluate our goals and strengthen our resolve.

Many therapists have recognised that over-stimulation can be pathogenic and have prescribed rest and freedom from social interaction as part of treatment. I believe that solitude can be a healing experience. Unfortunately, our culture teaches us that being alone is bad and that we *should* be constantly interacting with others. There is no disputing the fact that feelings of loneliness are unpleasant but, again, this depends very much on your perceptions. In a world that is crowded, noisy, overloaded with information and lacking in privacy, the antidote is solitude, stillness and time out. In an environment with fewer distractions, we can learn again to appreciate the important things we have put aside. Solitude, properly structured, may be used to overcome loneliness.

A well-established technique for turning loneliness into solitude is to challenge one's thinking. Such thoughts as 'nobody likes me', 'I can't make friends', 'I seem to be lacking in something', 'I can only see my life stretching into the future with no one being interested in me', are the thoughts that typically occur when a person feels lonely.

If you perceive yourself as lonely, the first step is to challenge that perception and change the dire need for human contact to a more appropriate preference and want. This does not mean that you are not going to set about developing social relationships and increasing the opportunities to meet people, but when you do, it will be clear to your new contacts that you are not desperately seeking them out. You can almost guarantee that as soon as you are perceived to be demanding that someone you have just met be your friend, he or she will generally react negatively and try to escape from you.

Men, women and loneliness

In working with people suffering from depression, I became aware that loneliness is a feeling they frequently described. The perception of being left alone is something that disturbs many people; the thought of a spouse leaving or dying is something that produces great anxiety.

Our culture instils in people an irrational *demand* that they have a partner all the time. Certainly, it is preferable if they do have one, but once it becomes a dire necessity, anxiety will almost certainly occur if the partner leaves or dies. Widows, for example, are statistically more numerous than widowers among older age groups and typically they miss (a) a companion with whom experiences and conditions are shared, (b) an escort in public for outings and social events, (c) another human being in the home (d) another human being to share the workload, (e) comfortable relations with old friends that are made difficult due to the absence of a partner.

Studies on men, women and marriage suggest that marriage is more an advantage for men than it is for women, and that being without a spouse is more of a liability for men than for women. This means that widows tend to cope better than widowers and manage more effectively the feelings of loneliness that occur. Women appear to be better than men at initiating and maintaining relationships with friends and relatives. It would also appear that women are generally more sociable than men as they get older.

Whenever a man or woman in a relationship is left alone, it then depends upon the individual's perception of the circumstances as to how he or she will react and deal with the aloneness. All too frequently in my work I hear the plea, 'I can't stand being alone', 'I am so frightened at the thought of having no one in the house with me any more.' The reality is that the majority of people cope with these circumstances quite well. It requires hard work to change feelings and patterns of behaviour that have developed over many years and, in many instances, is more difficult for older people than for the young, but it *is* possible. The value of friendships will be stressed later but there are a variety of techniques you can use to overcome your feelings of loneliness.

Planning

The chronically lonely person often shows many of the symptoms of depression, especially inactivity, lack of energy and loss of pleasure in activities that were once enjoyable. Many lonely people do not want to do anything if they have to do it alone. Nevertheless, research shows that taking part in activities, even when you are on your own, is often an essential first step in defeating loneliness. Simply converting feelings of isolation and loneliness to solitude is not enough. It is an important prerequisite to overcoming loneliness, but you must also make plans to start doing things again.

A daily, weekly, monthly, even yearly list of plans can be made. This does not have to be adhered to, but by simply doing this a lonely person can bring some structure into an often apparently fruitless existence because of the knowledge that certain things will happen the next day, the next week or the next month. Details of how to do this are given in Chapter 5, Self-organisation.

In my previous book, *Tactics for Changing Your life*, I included a list of 316 pleasant events devised by Professor Peter Lewinsohn of the University of Oregon that people can look at to select some activities they would find potentially pleasurable. The lonely client who seeks my advice would be encouraged to plan one enjoyable activity that would involve a potential friend. Depending on the client's willingness, it may be as simple as calling an old friend and having a conversation or as advanced as asking someone out to dinner.

Disputing negative thoughts

I urge people to write down any negative thoughts that occur to them spontaneously or as a result of some event and, in a column beside this, to write a counter-statement that will dispute the negative thought. For example:

Automatic negative thought	Balancing statement
'When I go out, people think I am dull and uninteresting. No one listens to me or will ever like me!'	'Some people may think that; too bad! However, unless I try to talk with others, listen to what they say and push myself to tell some interesting or humorous stories that I can even rehearse in advance, I will never know.'
'I have nothing to do alone, I will always be alone.'	'Not everyone who is alone is unhappy. I can turn loneliness into solitude, I can take steps to make friends in the future.'
'Time is running out for me, I will never meet anybody suitable.'	'Everyone has their own timetable. Some people don't get married until their sixties or seventies. I can still work at making friends and, no matter what happens, *i can stand it*.'

Making friends

First, plan and start a number of activities. Some examples are:

1. Going regularly to see a film.
2. Joining a tennis, health or other club.
3. Joining a political party or a community service organisation.
4. Enrolling in a cookery class, a car maintenance course or a language class that interests you.
5. Auditioning for an amateur theatrical group.

Then you can try initiating a number of non-intimate friendships, perhaps by casually approaching people in the group, saying to yourself, 'It will not be the end of the world if they do not respond to my approach.' This is making use of rational self-talk. Then you can keep on making approaches until a number of casual friendships have been established.

Conversational skills

The assertiveness training movement considers conversational skills very important. Many people seem to be born with the capacity to converse easily with others and therefore make many friends. Many others have learnt these skills.

Eye contact is important when you are talking to people and you wish to demonstrate an interest in what is being said. That does not mean staring at them intently until they recoil from you, but looking at their eyes when speaking, as well as nodding and smiling appropriately.

Open-ended questions are also important. These are questions that cannot be answered by a simple 'yes', 'no', or a grunt. They begin often with 'Who?', 'What?', 'When?', 'Where?', 'How?' or 'Why?' These queries tend to elicit more detailed information from another person. Consequently, they provide the opportunity for self-revelation. They can be the most comfortable type of question and lead to comfortable interaction between two or more people. These and other conversation skills are discussed in detail in Chapter 4, Assertiveness Training.

Obstacles to making friendships

People who often have difficulty starting friendships are those who have been involved in a previously intimate relationship that they have not been able to resolve satisfactorily. This is common among people recently divorced or separated and who cannot accept the fact that it has happened. Some of their typical self-talk might be:

- 'She left me because I don't know how to communicate.'
- 'I am unable to show my feelings.'
- 'I am a worthless person who nobody can love.'
- 'I don't think I can put myself on the line with anyone ever again.'

People with this type of problem can be helped by reviewing the relationship *objectively* and by writing down the events that occurred. Then they can challenge their automatic, negative and self-defeating thoughts that are preventing them from establishing new friendships.

Another group of people who avoid social contact are those who believe they are unattractive, unlikeable, boring or stupid. These over-generalisations often result from one or two previous experiences. Again, these conclusions can be challenged. Most people are able to establish relationships and friendships with others, even though they may not conform to television and magazine stereotypes with regard to looks and behaviour. Other people's perceptions of what is attractive are quite often different from our own. A man who is bald and short yet an excellent pianist and humorist would be attractive to many women, Yet *he* considers his shortness of stature and baldness as handicaps that will *never* allow him to make good friends and because of this attitude he will not attempt to make friends.

Developing intimate relationships

Once people have developed a number of transient and non-intimate frienships, they can concentrate on deepening a small number of these friendships.

Meeting the potentially right partner for an intense relationship, someone who shares the same interests, whose company you enjoy and who seems attractive to you may take a long time. That person will not just appear on your doorstep. It requires an effort to make social contacts using the skills described earlier. However, if you do, it is highly likely you will meet someone with whom you can develop an intimate relationship.

Other common ways in which men and women find partners include:

1. Making contact with old acquaintances and friends.
2. Asking a friend to arrange an outing with someone who seems compatible.

3. Approaching acquaintances and strangers who you think you might like in everyday situations, especially at work, on buses or trains, in cafes, pubs, parties.
4. Going on holidays or attending courses or singles dances where there are likely to be unattached people.

Deepening a relationship

Once you have found a desirable and suitable partner, you need to find ways to deepen the relationship. Intimacy is usually reached through a combination of self-disclosure, sexual contact and expressions of affection and caring. These require a genuine liking and positive feelings for the person as a whole. The conversational skills described earlier can be used to self-disclose and establish rapport. This can be enhanced by doing things together, sharing your feelings and enjoying each other's company.

There are many ways of expressing affection, such as buying gifts, writing letters, calling on the telephone, planning joint activities and tasks. Be aware of your partner's limitations and be realistic in your expectations. Acknowledge that you are dealing with another person who has the right to behave in certain ways, even though they may be annoying or irritating to you, and be prepared to compromise if you wish to sustain and continue the relationship.

Sexual problems

Many lonely people have difficulty initiating sexual intimacy, and relationships they have initiated may be low in sexual satisfaction. Sexual intimacy is a form of closeness and pleasure rather than 'a performance' with all the connotations associated with that word. Again, there is a great deal of information available from books but, more importantly, it is necessary to challenge and dispute the automatic negative thoughts that bring about these feelings. You may find *The Joy of Sex* by Alex Comfort published by Mitchell Beazley (1984) a useful book to read.

Unsatisfactory partners

Some lonely people have a tendency to choose unsatisfactory partners and thus have a history of relationships that end quickly or that are very difficult to maintain. Men and women who '*must*' have someone at their side, even if the partner is an alcoholic or violent or comes from a totally different educational/socio-economic background, are frequently disappointed. They 'fall in love' with one person after another without giving themselves an opportunity to evaluate the person and their suitability as a partner objectively. If you are such a person, spend time with partners who do not interest you much at first, yet seem to have other qualities that will prove to be important in the long run.

Low frustration tolerance

A common problem among people who feel lonely is their low tolerance of discomfort frustration. Most people find the initiating of a relationship with the opposite sex anxiety-provoking. You always feel safer with people you know and who accept you, rather than taking a chance with somebody you think might be interesting and with whom an intimate relationship may develop. This requires risk taking and the possibility of rejection which has been discussed in detail in *Tactics for Changing Your Life*.

Many people shy away from close relationships because they are afraid of losing their independence and privacy. They fear the partner will become too dependent upon them. Entrapment only exists when one person is afraid of expressing discomfort at the other person's demands; lovers are not obliged to meet *all* of each other's demands. The degree of intimacy, dependency and freedom are determined by negotiation.

Prevention of loneliness

One of our cultural preoccupations is with love relationships. The media, together with family and peer group pressure, help to create the intense need many people have for such relationships, and when they don't occur society suggests that somehow they are less than normal. I believe that people can live happily alone, provided they have a variety of friendships. I am convinced that the pressure to achieve exclusive one-to-one relationships should be relaxed and that friendships be given a much greater status.

Many of our social institutions are not designed to promote friendships. School classrooms, noisy and expensive singles bars or 'discos' which cater for a limited number of people are equally unsatisfactory. They provide no places where people can meet and chat informally. There are large numbers of older members of our community who have little opportunity to meet others informally.

The opportunities for informal social contact such as chatting in the launderette of a block of flats, or having a common lunchroom at work can set the stage for the beginning of new friendships. The development of relationships is further improved when people sometimes, out of necessity rather than choice, work together to accomplish shared goals. Such activities as special committees within organisations, amateur theatrical groups, community and work-based task forces, where people spend time working together, often present the opportunity for the development of further friendships. Cooperative interdependence creates a favourable climate for such contacts.

In contrast, competition is often a barrier to satisfying relationships. Schools are often competitive, unfriendly places. It would be valuable if, in the learning process, this could be changed so that children could learn to like and trust one another, not as an extra-curricular activity but in the course of everyday learning in subjects such as reading, writing and arithmetic.

Other kinds of community-based activities could be developed, ranging from social skills training for children in schools to programmes for groups known to be at high risk in the development of loneliness. These are children of divorced parents, widows and widowers and those who have newly arrived in the area to work or study, and for those from other parts of the world.

Evaluating loneliness

If you frequently experience feelings of loneliness, I suggest you fill in the following loneliness questionnaire developed by Dr Geoff Young. The value of this scale is that, after you begin working on your loneliness problems, you can re-test yourself and see if the score has dropped. You can also get further information from your answers; look at items No 4, 7, 8 and 11. If you circle higher numbers for most of these, this would suggest that you do not have many relationships at all. If this is correct, you will need to start with *initiating* relationships.

If you circle zero most often, then you probably have a number of casual relationships and your loneliness comes from difficulty in deepening them. This would be shown by higher scores on 1, 3, 6, 7, 10, 13 and 14. It would be best for you then to follow the techniques described in this chapter to *intensify and deepen* existing relationships.

Loneliness Scale

In this questionnaire are groups of statements. Pleased read each group of statements carefully, then pick out the one statement in each group that best describes you. Circle the number beside the statement you have picked. If several statements in the group seem to apply equally well, circle each one. Be sure to read *all* the statements in each group before making your choice.

1. 0 I have someone nearby I can really depend on and who cares about me.
   1 I'm not sure there's anyone nearby I can really depend on and who cares about me.
   2 There's no one anywhere I can really depend on and who cares about me right now.
   3 For several years I haven't had anyone I could really depend on and who cared about me.

2. 0 There is someone nearby who really understands me.
   1 I'm not sure there's anyone nearby who really understands me.
   2 There's no one who really understands me anywhere right now.
   3 For several years, no one has really understood me.

3. 0 I have someone nearby I could talk to about my private feelings.
   1 There's no one nearby I could talk to about my private feelings.
   2 There's no one I could talk to about my private feelings anywhere right now.
   3 For several years, I haven't had anyone I could talk to about my private feelings.

4. 0 I have a close group of friends nearby that I feel a part of.
   1 I don't feel part of any close group of friends nearby.
   2 I don't have a close group of friends anywhere.
   3 For several years, I haven't had a close group of friends.

5. 0 There is someone nearby who really needs me and wants my love.
   1 I'm not sure anyone nearby really needs me and wants my love.
   2 There isn't anyone who really needs me or wants my love right now.
   3 For several years, no one has really needed me or wanted my love.

6. 0 I have a lot in common with other people I know.
   1 I wish my values and interests, and those of other people I know, were more similar.
   2 I'm different from other people I know.

      3 I've felt different from other people for several
        years.

7. 0 When I want to do something for enjoyment, I can
        usually find someone to join me.
    1 Often I end up doing things alone even though I'd
        like to have someone to join me.
    2 There's no one right now I can go out and enjoy
        things with.
    3 There hasn't been anyone I could go out and enjoy
        things with for several years.

8. 0 There are no groups I'd really like to belong to that
        won't accept me.
    1 There is a group of people I know that I'd like to
        belong to but don't.
    2 It bothers me that there is a group of people I
        know right now who don't like me.
    3 For the past several years I've felt excluded by
        group(s) of people I've wanted to belong to.

9. 0 I rarely think about particular times in my life
        when my relationships seemed better.
    1 I sometimes wish my relationships now could be
        more like they were at another time in my life.
    2 I often wish my relationships now could be more
        like they were at another time in my life.
    3 I cannot stop thinking about how much better my
        relationships once were.

10. 0 I don't miss anyone in particular right now.
    1 I miss someone who isn't here now.
    2 I often think about a particular person I was close
        to.
    3 I cannot stop thinking about someone I lost.

11 0 I feel like a part of a 'team' with the people I work
        with.

1 I am not employed at the present time.
2 There is little team feeling where I work.
3 There is a team feeling among the people I work with, but I do not feel I fit in.
4 Most of the people I work with don't like me.

12. 0 I can usually talk freely to close friends about my thoughts and feelings.
1 I have some difficulty talking to close friends about my thoughts and feelings.
2 I feel as though my thoughts and feelings are bottled up inside.
3 I cannot seem to communicate with anyone.

13. 0 The important people in my life have not let me down.
1 I'm still disappointed at someone I thought I could trust.
2 As I look back at my life many people I trusted have let me down.
3 I find I can't trust anyone any more.

14. 0 I can almost always enjoy myself when I am alone.
1 I can sometimes enjoy myself alone.
2 I can rarely enjoy myself alone.
3 I can never really enjoy myself when I am alone.

15. 0 I rarely wish that my relationships could be more like other people's.
1 I sometimes wish that I could have relationships that satisfied me the way other people's relationships satisfy them.
2 I often wish that I could have relationships that satisfied me the way other people's relationships satisfy them.
3 I cannot stop comparing the satisfaction other people get from their relationships with my own lack of satisfaction.

16. 0 There is someone I am physically intimate with now on a regular basis.
    1 I am not physically intimate with anyone now on a regular basis.
    2 I am often disturbed that I am not physically intimate with someone on a regular basis now.
    3 I have not been physically intimate with anyone on a regular basis for several months.

17. 0 I haven't felt lonely during the past week (including today).
    1 I've felt somewhat lonely during the past week (including today).
    2 I've felt very lonely during the past week (including today).
    3 I could barely stand the loneliness during the past week (including today).

18. 0 Loneliness has never been a real problem for me.
    1 There have been times in my life when I've felt quite lonely, but not during the past few months.
    2 I've felt lonely regularly during the past months.
    3 I've felt lonely for several years.
    4 I've always felt lonely.

This scale is reprinted with the permission of Dr Jeffrey E Young, PhD, of the Department of Psychiatry, Columbia University.

References

J E Young, 'Loneliness, Depression and Cognitive Therapy: Theory and Application', pages 379–406 in: *Loneliness: A Source Book of Current Theory Research and Therapy*, Eds L A Peplau and D Perlman, Wiley, New York (1982)

J Meer, 'Loneliness', *Psychology Today*, Vol 19, 28 (1985)

P Russianoff, *Women in Crisis*, Human Science Publications, USA (1981)

R Albert and M Emmons, *Your Perfect Right*, Impact Press, USA (1974)

M J Smith, *When I say No I Feel Guilty'*, Bantam Books (1973)

A D Kidman, *Tactics for Changing Your Life*, Kogan Page (1989)

R S Weiss, *Loneliness: The Experience of Emotional and Social Isolation*, MIT Press, Cambridge, Mass (1975)

CHAPTER 4
Assertiveness Training

Definition

Assertive behaviour is interpersonal behaviour involving the honest and relatively straightforward expression of thoughts and feelings. It is socially appropriate and when a person is behaving assertively the feelings and welfare of others are taken into account.

It is important to distinguish between non-assertive (passive), assertive and aggressive behaviour.

Assertive behaviour communicates feelings, beliefs and needs directly and clearly, while non-assertion and aggression are indirect forms of communication.

Non-assertive behaviour implies that you allow the needs of others to override your own needs. It includes deference and agreeing with the opinions of others because you are fearful or want to please them. Generally, you do not achieve your objectives because of the inability to communicate effectively.

Aggressive behaviour is the expression of needs and demands at the expense of others. It implies a desire to injure and hurt people who do not agree with your demands or beliefs.

Components of assertive behaviour

The following characteristics have been observed in people who behave assertively.

1. *Eye contact*. Looking directly at another person when speaking to them is a good way of letting them know that you are sincere in what you are saying.

2. *Body posture.* The significance of your message to others will be increased if you face the person, sit or stand appropriately close, lean towards them and hold your head up.

3. *Gestures.* A message accentuated with appropriate gestures takes on added emphasis. Suitable facial expressions are also important; it would be inappropriate to be smiling when you are expressing sympathy.

4. *Voice tone, inflection and volume.* A whispered monotone will seldom convince another person that you mean business, while shouting abuse will arouse their defences and block communication. A level, well-modulated statement is convincing without being intimidating.

5. *Timing.* Spontaneous expression of feelings would be preferable, but judgement is necessary to select an appropriate occasion. If you were discussing an employee's continual lateness for work, it would be better to speak to that person privately rather than in front of a group of colleagues where the employee may feel the need to respond defensively.

6. *Content.* Although *what* is said is clearly important, it is not as important as many people believe. *How, when* and *where* the words are said are crucial. 'You silly fool, you forgot to give me that message', said in a snarling, demeaning tone with angry looks compared with the same words said in a neutral tone with a calm appearance may convey the same information but will produce an enormous difference in reaction. It is the interpretation of the words by the listener that will determine the response. The first method may be effective but will more than likely create resentment towards you and a desire to get even with you for name-calling, whereas the second method will remind the person of his omission, the upset it has caused you and the need to write messages down.

Expressing needs and feelings

- How do you pay a compliment or express affection?
- How do you receive a compliment or expressions of affection from others?

- How do you ask for something or refuse someone's request?
- How do you tell someone to change his way of doing something?
- How do you express annoyance at someone else's behaviour?

These are all problems that people face and there are many ways of dealing with them.

Assertiveness training teaches people to express their emotions to others as spontaneously and as honestly as they can, especially their positive feelings. It is important to be personal and to use 'I' statements. Some examples in everyday situations are as follows.

- 'I can see that you put a lot of effort into preparing this report so it could be clearly understood by every member of the department. I appreciate your efforts.'
- 'I just wanted to tell you how much your encouragement has meant to me. It has helped me to feel more confident of myself. I am doing things I wouldn't have dreamt of last year. Thanks.'
- 'I love you.'
- 'When I hear you laugh, it makes me feel good.'

We often assume that people understand our appreciation of their efforts or our affection for them. Unfortunately signals and messages are often confused or blurred and it is important to state and re-state the good things that we think about others, be they our spouse, children or colleagues. This also reinforces the helpful actions of people and increases the chance that they will continue acting in that way.

It is equally important to express negative feelings, using 'I' statements. Brooding about the behaviour of others and bottling up resentment and disappointment will intensify these feelings and generate more self-defeating thoughts. To prevent yourself becoming more and more upset, the first line of action is to dispute these thoughts when they arise to reduce the feelings of hostility, depression or guilt. This will not eliminate them, but will make them manageable.

If you are angry with another person's actions and have reduced your feelings to appropriate annoyance, you now need to take some action and express your feelings to that person. For instance, your neighbour seems to choose early Sunday mornings to use his chain-saw to cut logs. The non-assertive approach would be to say nothing to the neighbour but fume and complain to your family and generally have an unpleasant morning. The aggressive reaction would be to shout abuse at the neighbour over the fence or ring him up to say you are calling the police. This would probably sour relations for a long time.

The assertive option would be to approach the neighbour in a friendly manner and tell him clearly that the noise of the chain-saw at that time of the day is causing some problems as you usually sleep in. You could then suggest that perhaps this work could be done later in the morning or at some more appropriate time or that it could be done further away from your bedroom window.

Rather than serving your neighbour with an ultimatum that unless he stops the noise you will call the police, a number of alternatives are presented. There is always the possibility, generally remote, that the person will be unreceptive, rude and ignore you. Again, using appropriate self-talk first, you can state your position clearly and that further action will be taken either by approaching the local council or the police to try to resolve the problem. This is known as escalation and I will explain this in detail later.

The important issue here is the context – how the information is conveyed. Words are symbols and it is our interpretation of these verbal signals that will determine our reactions. Sometimes a carefully worded letter may be the means of dealing with the problem. Another option is a telephone call, prior to which you have jotted down a number of points and your replies to possible responses.

Handling aggression in yourself and others

When people, in your opinion, behave aggressively or unfairly towards you that is often the signal for an intense anger response. In many instances it is better to ignore such behaviour. If you are driving along the main road and another driver blows his horn, yells abuse at you and then speeds away, it is better to let him go rather than to take off in hot pursuit and risk an accident and injury. The appropriate self-talk to use would be, 'Why should I let someone else's stupid behaviour put my life in jeopardy?'

Another situation may be at work or at home when harsh words have been said to you. An assertive response would be to listen to what was being said, no matter how difficult that may be, as there may be an element of truth in it. You can then express your feelings firmly, intensely and even in a raised voice using the 'I' statement technique: 'I am so annoyed with your failure to listen to my side of the story. I believe I acted fairly but I was mistaken. Shouting at me will not help. I'd like to come back in 20 minutes, when the situation is calmer, and try to work things out.'

In this example you have re-interpreted the provocative event so that you are aroused and will take action that is a positive attribute of anger, but you are not out of control and your actions are likely to help you achieve your goal of correcting your mistakes and not souring your relationship with others.

Implementing assertive procedures

Behaviour rehearsal

The most commonly used assertiveness training technique is behaviour rehearsal. In front of a mirror or with another person, such as a therapist or a friend, you imagine a scene in your mind and act out the relevant interpersonal interactions. The problem may be something as simple as going to a supermarket queue and asking the person at the top if you may go ahead of them as you want to buy only one item. This is rehearsed several times and then done as an assignment, perhaps three times a week. Each time you do it, whether you are successful (which you most probably will be) or not, you reward yourself in some way perhaps by buying yourself a small gift.

The minimal effective response

Assertion means expressing appropriate feelings. Deciding whether a particular action is appropriate is a matter of social judgement. When expressing feelings such as hurt or annoyance, a good rule is to implement the *minimal effective response*. This is behaviour that would normally accomplish the goal by expressing the minimal negative emotion and effort. The following annoying situations with minimal effective responses frequently occur:

1. A petrol station attendant fails to clean your windscreen when he is supposed to. 'I wonder if you would mind cleaning the windscreen as it is rather dirty.'
2. A waiter charges you for a drink you didn't have. 'I believe you have made an error in the bill; would you mind checking it again?'
3. A friend continually interrupts you. 'I am sure you don't realise this, but sometimes I get a little flustered when you interrupt.' (With a friendly smile.)

Escalation

In any of the previous situations be prepared to encounter unresponsiveness or hostility and to escalate your response to achieve your goal. It is important to keep escalation within the realms of plausibility and to remind yourself that unpleasant counter-responses are rare. Many people are non-assertive because they catastrophise about what would happen if they acted in a determined way and are fearful of the consequences.

The following is an example of escalation dealing with people who are talking during a film.

Complainant. 'I wonder if you could please be a little quieter, I am having difficulty hearing the film.'
After five minutes of silence, the chatter resumes.
(First order escalation.)

Complainant. 'Look, would you please be a little quieter, I simply cannot hear the film.'
Spokesman for chatterers. 'Sorry.'
(Silence for the remainder of the film.)

You may wish to extend this into a second order escalation.

The second complaint is met with the response: 'Hell, what are you so uptight about,' followed by continued chatter.
You reply: 'If you don't keep quiet, I shall call the manager.'

This could be followed by the counter response: 'Okay, okay!' and there would be silence for the remainder of the film or, 'This character is getting on my nerves, let's leave.'

Non-assertive people often feel they will be embarrassed by being assertive. They often think as follows:

'What will people think if there is a scene?'
'I can't stand a public argument.'

Such thoughts are really irrational demands that strangers must approve of your actions in expressing your valid rights. This can be challenged mentally by saying, 'So what if some people (who I don't even know) object to me asserting my rights – too bad!'

Another fear is that the other person may resort to abuse or physical violence during an escalated encounter. The likelihood of this happening is very much lower than you think. It has been found that individuals who behave in a bullying manner usually succumb to verbal assertiveness so the interchange rarely reaches the point of physical threats or violence. It is important during any exchanges not to indulge in personal insults.

Developing conversational skills

Most of us have experienced the uncomfortable feeling of being in a conversation full of pauses where people are groping or straining to think of something to say just to keep the conversation going. When this happens, there is a tendency to become anxious and this reduces the flow of conversation and makes things appear worse than they are.

It is important to decide how you want to present yourself in conversation with others and what it is that you want to achieve from a conversation. Do you want to convey information as efficiently as possible? Do you want to find out more about a particular person and let him know more about your interests? Or do you just want to enjoy a verbal exchange with a stranger who you will probably never see again?

Open-ended questions

Questions are often the best way to initiate and sustain a conversation. The purpose of asking questions during a conversation is usually to discover areas of mutual interest. An open-ended question is one that will allow the other person to share information easily. The following are some examples of closed and open-ended questions.

- *Closed question:* 'Do you work in this department too?'
  Answer: 'Yes.'

  Closed question: 'Do you like it?'
  Answer: 'It's okay.'

  Closed question: 'Have you been here long?'
  Answer: 'Four years.'

  Closed question: 'Do you live around here?'
  Answer: 'Yes, in Newport.'

  Closed question: 'Do you go to discos very often?'
  Answer: 'Sometimes.'

  Closed question: 'Isn't it hot in here?'
  Answer: 'Yes.'

Closed question:	'Are you as bored as I am?'
Answer:	'Yes.'

● *Open-ended question:* 'Where do you work?'
Answer: 'At the hospital.'

Open-ended question: 'What do you do there?'
Answer: 'I am a nurse.'

Open-ended question: Really! What ward do you work in?'
Answer: 'I am not in the wards, I teach other nurses physiology and biological sciences.'

Open-ended question: 'You sound as though you enjoy your work. What is it you like about it so much?'
Answer: 'I really enjoy working with people and I find the teaching environment stimulating. Sometimes I get so involved with the lectures and students that we often run over time and other lecturers are outside the door waiting to come in.'

Open-ended question: 'Why did you leave the wards to get into the teaching field?'
Answer: 'It happened quite by accident. I was working in the intensive care ward where we had groups of nursing students coming around, and for some reason it usually fell to me to explain the details of the cases. I enjoyed this so much, particularly explaining the biological background of the conditions, that I decided to take training in this area and got my diploma in nursing education.'

You will notice that much more information resulted from 'What?' and 'How?' as opposed to 'Do you?' or 'Are you?' Not everyone wants to talk about their job, nor are all jobs interesting. The point is that open-ended questions give others a greater opportunity to share what is interesting to them.

Disclosing information about yourself

Open-ended questions will enable you to stay focused on one area of conversation for a longer period without having to ask a lot of questions or make clever remarks. Some people work much too hard at carrying on a conversation.

Apart from asking the appropriate questions, you might share something about yourself that is related to the topic of discussion. You should use this technique carefully. We are all familiar with the person who seeks to dominate a conversation by talking about personal achievements and qualifications. This will stifle a mutually pleasurable conversation and generate resentment. If you have a tendency to do this, practise pausing more often so that others can come in on the conversation, and think ahead about what you are saying. Do not be over-anxious about how people are reacting to you – the more you practise your questions and anticipated responses, the more you will expand your range of conversation. Thinking ahead about how you will conduct yourself is not artificial if you wish to reflect your true self.

The following example is part of a conversation between strangers at a party.

Jane.   'What do you like about living in Brighton?'
Peter.   'I love it. I live near the beach as I like to swim and to fish.' (Self-disclosure.)
Jane.   'That sounds great. I thought about living near the beach but decided on a flat nearer the centre. It is a little noiser, but I enjoy being near the shops and the station. (Free information and self-disclosure.)

This brief example shows the use of an open-ended question and self-disclosure.

Re-stating and highlighting

There may be times when you don't have an open-ended question in mind and you don't wish to say anything about yourself as you are interested in what the other person has said and would like to hear more. Therefore, highlight something the other person has already said by responding in the following way:

Stranger.   'I am a teacher at a primary school. Young children are so much fun to work with. They are so open and so curious.'

Highlight.   'You really like working with these kids?'

Stranger.   'Yes, they want to know everything. I really have to be on my toes to keep up with them.'

Highlight.   'They obviously keep you very busy in the classroom.'

As you can see, when you highlight you must listen attentively to what other people are saying and evaluate their feelings as your interest reflects their communication. As well as encouraging further conversation, such highlight responses let people know you are listening and interested in what they are saying.

Changing the conversation

When you are talking with someone you want to be with but are not interested in the immediate conversation, there are ways of changing the subject. Being direct and honest is the best way.

Jill and John worked in the same office and office politics were often discussed. On one occasion when John was speaking of one of the latest pieces of gossip, Jill realised she would prefer not to discuss this now so she asserted her wish to change the topic when John said, 'I'd almost forgotten to mention that the Chairman of the board was seen ...', by replying, 'John, I know we often talk about what's going on in the office, but right now I'd rather leave it because there's been a lot of tension lately. What did you think of the tennis last night?'

If you want to change the topic or the direction of the conversation you don't have to break into the middle of it. Most people will pause when they talk or eventually there is an end to a story or the completion of a point. This is the best time to express your preference for another subject as it is the most considerate way of doing so for both yourself and the speaker.

Ending conversations

Ending a conversation is a separate and sometimes difficult step in itself. You may wish to end a conversation as you are not interested in either the person or the topic, or you may feel that the conversation is becoming forced and you want to end it at a comfortable point. It is better to end a conversation before you run out of something to say or get stuck with an unwanted topic. Knowing that you can always stop a conversaton when you want to will help you to relax and provides a greater sense of control.

Non-verbal signals include moving away slightly and a reduction in eye contact and nodding. You may then express your legitimate preference to end the conversation:

- 'I am going to get a drink and circulate a little. It's been nice talking to you.'
- 'I see Bob over there. Excuse me as I have been looking for him for some time.'

If the person is someone you like and will seek out in the future, you could say, 'I'll see you again later' as this is both honest and appropriate.

It is important to remember that a great amount of a person's perception of you is communicated non-verbally. A dull tone, a bored look, signs of irritation or annoyance can have a very negative impact on the person with whom you are conversing. It is better to express your preference to finish a conversation in a pleasant, clear and informative manner that does not put the other person down and make you responsible for hurt feelings.

Defensive methods

A very important part of assertiveness training, especially if you are non-assertive, is to learn how to protect yourself when you are being unfairly criticised, pressured or taken advantage. The techniques described below can be applied when you have attempted by a clear, honest statement of fact to indicate that your needs or your value as a person is not being respected.

Disarming anger

How should a wife react when her husband continues to abuse her and call her names after he has been told clearly that this is upsetting her and that she sees it as most unfair. Should she abuse him back, throw things at him or pack up and leave?

In this situation, disarming anger can be a very useful technique and, in some cases, may save a person from physical injury. The method is a form of negotiation offered by an assertive person to someone who is behaving in an extremely angry fashion bordering on physical violence.

Husband.	'You are so stupid, when will you get things done on time?'
Wife.	'You are really angry, I am not sure what particular things you are referring to. Why can't you sit down and we can talk about it?' (Clear and honest communication.)
Husband.	'Talk about it! I'm not sure you're smart enough to listen to a simple sentence in English! I want you to have things done when I need them!'
Wife.	'Look, I want to talk about this, but I really can't when I'm being screamed at. Sit down and let's talk about it calmly.' (Clear and honest communication.)
Husband.	'I *am* calm, you idiot! Can't you do *anything* right?'
Wife.	'I am willing to talk to you about this if you will sit down and stop screaming at me.'
Husband.	'What if I don't want to stop?'
Wife.	'Then let's talk about it later when you are not so angry. I want to get this settled but only if you are not yelling at me.' (Negotiation offer.)
Husband.	'I want to settle this right now.'
Wife.	'Then please sit down and stop yelling so we can settle it.'

Husband. 'OK, I am sitting and I am not yelling. Why wasn't my shirt ironed?'

The wife has managed to diffuse some of her husband's anger and they are in a position to communicate and the wife can account for her actions.

Broken record

This technique can be used in situations where you are being harassed by someone to do something you do not want to do. For example, a salesperson continues with a high pressure pitch even though you have stated clearly that you are not interested in buying the product he is selling. Do you slam the door in the salesperson's face, do you lie or how do you get him out of your house?

The 'broken record' is the continuous repetition of a person's feelings or main point. No issues are dealt with in the conversation other than the particular point being stressed. This person sounds like a 'broken record' repeating over and over again his position in as concise a statement as possible.

Here is an example of its use with the salesperson:

Salesman. 'I would like to show you these home-cleaning products I am selling.'

Customer. 'No thank you, I am not interested in buying any of those things today.'

Salesman. 'I really have some outstanding products to offer.'

Customer. 'That may be true but I have all the cleaning items I need at present. (Honest and clear communication.)

Salesman. 'Do you have any family?'

Customer. 'The point is, I am not interested in buying any items today.' (Broken record.)

Salesman. 'Well then, is your wife home, she may be interested?'

Customer. 'I don't want any of these products.' (Broken record.)

Salesman. 'Wouldn't you like her to make her own choice as she probably cleans the house?'

Customer.	'I don't want any of these products.' (Broken record.)

(There is no law that says you have to answer questions put to you, in this case by the salesman, and you have the perfect right not to answer.)

Salesman.	'I have told you that 50 per cent of the profits from these products goes to medical research. Aren't you concerned about the health of your children?'
Customer.	'The point is, I am not interested in buying any of your products today.'
Salesman.	'OK, would you take this brochure and think about it?'
Customer.	'Yes, I will take the brochure.' (Negotiated ending.)
Salesman.	'Thank you.'
Customer.	'You're welcome.'

Selective ignoring

Selective ignoring requires a conscious decision to attend to the specific content from one individual and not to comment on other matters. An assertive person does not reply to unfair or abusive interactions but instead replies only to statements that are not destructive, guilt-producing or unjust. The abusive person is met with silence when he is being unjust. Non-verbal techniques can also be used; for instance, head nodding is a particular reinforcing non-verbal cue to a speaker. When the undesirable content is presented by the abuser, the recipient remains silent with no head nodding. The following is an example of this technique in action. A woman has met a friend for lunch.

Woman.	'Hello!'
Friend.	'Hi! How are you?'
Woman.	'I'm fine, how are you?'
Friend.	'Actually, I'm feeling a bit down.'
Woman.	'That's no good, what is the problem?'
Friend.	'You haven't phoned me since you moved to your new flat. I suppose you're just too busy for old friends.'

Woman.	'You know I'm very fond of you. However, what with moving, part-time studies and an exam coming up, I needed to go underground for a while.'
Friend.	'Are you saying that I am not worth the time for a phone call or that you cannot take a couple of minutes to ring me once in a while?'
Woman.	'I don't really want to speak like this but I feel you are criticising me and I know that if this conversation continues we will end up arguing so I am not going to say any more if you continue in this vein.'
Friend.	'I'm only criticising you for your own good. If a friend can't be honest with you, who can?'
Woman.	(Silence.)
Friend.	'Are you still going out with that hopeless fellow?'
Woman.	(Silence.)
Friend.	'I asked if you are still going out with that hopeless fellow?'
Woman.	(Silence.)
Friend.	'Why aren't you answering me?'
Woman.	'I don't like your criticism. I feel that as a friend and equal I am capable of making my own decisions and choices as to who I go out with.' (Clear and honest communication.)
Friend.	'If that were true, you would be married by now. After all, how many girls are still unmarried and studying at the age of 33?'
Woman.	(Silence.)
Friend.	'If you aren't going to answer me, what is there left to talk about?' (Offer of negotiation.)
Woman.	'Would you like to hear about my promotion at work?' (Return offer of negotiation.)
Friend.	'Oh, you got a promotion, tell me about it?' (Acceptance.)

Guilt reduction

We often feel guilty when we don't accede to the wishes of

'significant others' in our lives – parents, children, spouse, friends and colleagues.

Unfortunately, many people experience intense guilt because of what they perceive to be irresponsible actions by themselves and, as a result, they feel and behave in a self-defeating way and frequently say 'I'm sorry' almost automatically.

With the guilt reduction technique it is important to learn to accept responsibility for your actions but to drop the 'I'm sorry' statements and to admit error without compromising dignity.

Let us assume that a staff member is late for an office meeting and the chairman who is the manager comments:

Manager. 'You are late!'

Member. 'Yes, I know. I apologise for being late but I did not realise how late it was when I left the house.'

Manager. 'I do not like excuses. I feel it is very important to start these sessions on time – together.'

Member. 'It was not intended as an excuse. I was telling you what happened. I shall be here on time next week.'

There is nothing wrong with the words 'I'm sorry', but they are so often used automatically by people when they do not really mean to apologise but feel an excessive amount of guilt. It is for this reason that I suggest using them as little as possible.

Fog

This is a technique in which one takes on an extremely passive role in the interaction. The assertive person using the 'fog' appears to agree that the other individual 'may be right' or 'is probably correct', but does not specifically state that the other person *is* correct only that he *may be* correct. The assertive person never agrees to change.

'The 'fog' technique can be useful in interrupting a chronic nag. For example, a man is nagging a woman about her driving:

Man. 'You really are a poor driver. You are driving really badly again and I have asked you so many times not to drive that way.'

Woman.	'We have been through this before. You know I don't appreciate it when you constantly criticise my driving. You asked me to drive you to work today.' (Clear and honest communication.)
Man.	'But you look at me when you talk and take your eyes off the road. You should not have the radio on as it probably distracts you.'
Woman.	'You are probably right. Perhaps I shouldn't have the radio on.' (Begins the 'fog' here.)
Man.	'Then you agree that you are a bad driver!'
Woman.	'You may be right.' (Fog.)
Man.	'Don't look in my direction when you talk to me.'
Woman.	(Glancing in his direction.) 'You're probably right, I should not look at you when I'm driving.' (Fog.)
Man.	'But you are still doing it, so why are you saying I may be right?'
Woman.	'I'm not really agreeing with you, I just don't want to be nagged any more. Let's talk about something else.' (Clear and honest communication.)

When to use assertiveness training

It is important to think of assertiveness training as a tool that can be used on appropriate occasions. You do not *have* to be assertive in *all* situations. It is often appropriate just to listen to people when they have a problem or are trying to get some help. It may be more appropriate not to use assertiveness techniques with a neurotic spouse, boss or colleague whose behaviour is well known to you. If you *suddenly* become assertive, this may precipitate trouble. I recently heard of a case where an employee who had been working with a difficult manager for a long time took an assertiveness training course and then decided to assertively express objections to the manager about his behaviour and manners. The employee was dismissed on the spot.

Use your judgement when to employ these techniques, and in the majority of cases, they will produce the desired outcome. Start slowly, using the exercises that have been described earlier and build up your confidence and skills over time.

Exercises

Exercise 1. Developing your style
Select two or three people to approach at different times and decide in advance how you would like to relate to them.

(a) What is your goal?
(b) How do you want to present yourself generally?
(c) What will you do non-verbally to present yourself?
(d) What underlying need to impress might get in the way?

You don't have to have a pre-determined script but you should give some thought to each of the four questions above. After you have asked yourself these questions, evaluate your behaviour in terms of your answers.

1. Did you do what you said you would?
2. Did you like the way you did it?
3. What would you change next time?

Exercise 2. Expressing positive feelings
In each of the following situations, consider how you would express your positive feelings.

Situation. A friend has unexpectedly dropped off a record you have been wanting to get and hear for some time.

You say: ....

....

....

Situation. You have been feeling very upset about some problem at work and a friend has been listening and helping you sort out your feelings. After talking to your friend for a while you feel much better.

You say: ....

....

....

Exercise 3. Editing your comments
For each of the following situations, write down how you could edit your thoughts to make assertive instead of aggressive statements.

Situation. A neighbour has just parked his car near your drive so that you can only get your car in and out with difficulty. You have asked him not to do this. You think to yourself 'He is such a fool doing this after I have asked him not to. I am going to give him a piece of my mind.'

Editing comments: ....

....

....

Situation. Your boss asks you to run a personal errand during your lunch hour. You think, 'I am not a servant, I don't get paid to do that work, I should not be asked to do that!'

Editing comments: ....

....

....

Situation. Someone on your local Neighbourhood Watch Committee has just made what you consider to be a ridiculous suggestion. You think, 'What a stupid idea, he should know better than that!'

Editing comments: ....

....

....

Exercise 4. Beginning and ending conversations

(a) With a friend, practise initiating conversations as though the friend was a stranger or a brief acquaintance. Try various approaches, using a combination of statements and open-ended questions.

(b) Assume you have been talking with someone for a while and would like to end the conversation. Practise ending the conversation without demeaning the other person or making up excuses. Try several possible statements.

(c) At least twice during the week initiate a conversation and end a conversation (not necessarily one you initiated). Evaluate what happens in all four cases and what you might have done differently.

The Gambrill and Richey Assertion Inventory

This Inventory is a self-report questionnaire so that you can assess both your degree of discomfort in a hypothetical assertive situation in one column, and the likelihood of actually behaving this way in the second column. Indicate your degree of discomfort or anxiety in the space provided before each situation listed. For example, in situation 5, if you find it very difficult to apologise when you are fault, you would put a 5. Use the following scale to indicate the degree of discomfort:

1 = none
2 = a little
3 = a fair amount
4 = much
5 = very much

Then go over the list a second time and indicate *after* each item the probability or likelihood of your behaving this way. For example, in situation 5, if you rarely apologise when you are at fault you would put a 4. Use the following scale to indicate the probability of your responding that way:

1 = always do it
2 = usually do it
3 = do it about half the time
4 = rarely do it
5 = never do it

Last, indicate the situations you would like to handle more assertively by placing a circle around the situation number.

Note: It is important to cover your discomfort ratings (located in front of the situations) while indicating response probability. Otherwise, one rating may contaminate the other and a realistic assessment of your behaviour is unlikely. To correct this, place a piece of paper over your discomfort ratings.

Add up the total numerical values for each situation. On average, the mean discomfort scores range from 95 to 100. Do the same for your response probability column. Average scores there range from 100 to 105.

Degree of discomfort	Situation	Response probability
4	1. Turn down a request to borrow your car.	2
2	2. Compliment a friend.	2
4	3. Ask a favour of someone.	4
2	4. Resist sales pressure.	2
5	5. Apologise when you are at fault.	1
2	6. Turn down a request for a meeting or a date.	3
4	7. Admit fear and request consideration.	3
4	8. Tell a person you are intimately involved with when he/she says or does something that bothers you.	4
4	9. Ask for a rise.	4
2	10. Admit ignorance in some area.	3

33 .

28

Degree of discomfort	Situation	Response probability
3	11. Turn down a request to borrow money.	2
2	12. Ask personal questions.	4
2	13. Turn off a talkative friend.	3
2	14. Ask for constructive criticism.	4
4	15. Initiate a conversation with a stranger.	4
1	16. Compliment a person you are romantically involved with or interested in.	2
4	17. Request a meeting or a date with someone.	4
5	18. Your initial request for a meeting is turned down; ask the person again at a later time.	4
4	19. Admit confusion about a point under discussion and ask for clarification.	4
3	20. Apply for a job.	2
4	21. Ask whether you have offended someone.	4
4	22. Tell someone that you like him/her.	4
4	23. Request expected service when it is not forthcoming, eg in a restaurant.	3
4	24. Discuss openly with someone his/her criticism of your behaviour.	5
4	25. Return defective items, eg in a store or restaurant.	3
3	26. Express an opinion that differs from that of the person you are talking to.	3
49 33		55

Degree of discomfort	Situation	Response probability
1	27. Resist sexual overtures when you are not interested.	5
5	28. Tell someone when you feel he/she has done something that is unfair to you.	4
1	29. Accept a date.	3
2	30. Tell someone good news about yourself.	2
2	31. Resist pressure to drink.	1
4	32. Resist a significant person's unfair demand.	4
2	33. Resign from a job.	5
1	34. Resist pressure to take drugs.	1
2	35. Discuss openly with someone his/her criticism of your work.	4
3	36. Request the return of borrowed items.	4
2	37. Receive compliments.	3
3	38. Continue to converse with someone who disagrees with you.	3
4	39. Tell a friend or someone with whom you work when he/she says or does something that bothers you.	4
5	40. Ask a person who is annoying you in public to stop.	4

37
82

References

R E Alberti and M L Emmons, *Your Perfect Right: A Guide to Assertive Behaviour*, Impact Press, USA (1974)

D C Rimm and J C Masters, Behaviour Therapy, Chapter 3, *Assertive Training*, Academic Press (1979)

M J Smith, *When I Say No I Feel Guilty*, Bantam (1973)

CHAPTER 5
Self-organisation

Once your thinking has been challenged and your intense feelings of anxiety, depression or guilt have been brought under control, then it is important to work on that part of the external world that you can change. This is the 'A' in the A → B → C model (on page 14). While a relaxed approach to problems is desirable, it is pointless for people to become relaxed incompetents. Initially, identify and write down the goals you want to achieve. This means making a list as lists are important to the achievement of objectives. Thus people need a place to work, particularly in the home – a desk or table top where they have pen, paper, folders and other materials that are necessary for planning.

We all need to take responsibility for our actions and this requires managing ourselves and negotiating with others. Managing ourselves requires management of our time. One person cannot do all the things they feel they 'should' be doing; often this means responding to the never-ending demands of superiors, spouse, children, colleagues or friends. Management of a *home* is as important as management of an *office*. Home management is generally done by women who have the enormous task of planning and scheduling the feeding, clothing and leisure activities of a family, but men are equally in need of home management.

Time management is learning how to decide what activities are important to achieve your prepared goals and how to go about doing them. It is also about deciding what *not* to do. It does not mean trying to cram more and more activities into a day, but rather completing the desired tasks and setting aside time for relaxation and enjoyment. This is an essential feature of time management. It also allows people to schedule new and interesting activities into their lives.

Goals and priorities

Lists

The first step in managing yourself and your time more effectively is to write a list of goals. Making several goal lists is recommended and these can be divided further into work and non-work related goals. Alan Lakein in his book, *How to Get Control of Your Time and Your Life*, suggests that you prepare a lifetime goals list at various times during your life, starting now. Ask yourself what long-term goals are important to you. Now take a few minutes to list these long-term goals on paper. Phrase these in a general way and include personal, family, social, career, financial and community goals. Make your list as inclusive as possible. Don't be afraid to include such wishes as walking the Himalayas, taking a year off, chartering a yacht, losing weight by jogging each day. There is nothing wrong with uncensored fantasies.

On another sheet of paper, list your short-term goals – those things you would like to achieve in the next two to three years. Again, let your imagination go to work. These lists are for your eyes only; they are drafts and can be revised as frequently as you wish.

Setting priorities

You now have lists of goals, short and long term, but listing goals is not enough. You now have to decide the *priority* of these goals. Goals might include such things as:

(a) being promoted to district manager
(b) increasing sales by 20 per cent
(c) improving the relationship with my spouse
(d) reducing my mortgage by £5000
(e) learning a new language.

To set priorities you can use the ABC system, where A is a high-value goal, B a medium-value goal and C a low-value goal. Go to your list and mark each goal with an appropriate letter. If you find you have a number of A goals, you will need to divide these further into A1, A2 and A3. Ultimately, you will come up with two or three goals that are top priority at work and at home. These lists are not carved in stone so they can be altered and should be reviewed regularly, at least once or twice a year or more often depending on changes in circumstances. I suggest you re-write your list if you change jobs, get married or become a parent. Some people use their birthday as a reminder to re-write their goals list.

Steps to achieve goals

The next step is attaining the goals or objectives. It doesn't just happen; you need to take another sheet of paper and list the steps to be taken to achieve your selected goal. By doing this you gain a much clearer perspective of where you are going. One of the great problems for many people is that their objectives are not sufficiently clear. People have broad ideas about what they want to do or where they want to go but objectives often overlap and become confused. This technique will help you to clarify your objectives and in planning activities both at work and at home in the light of these written goals.

I wish to emphasise the importance of keeping a folder containing these lists and to re-read, re-write and upgrade these objectives regularly.

Management

My definition of management is achieving objectives through others. A good manager with leadership qualities knows how to influence people in order to accomplish desired objectives. These principles apply in the home as well as in the office.

Delegating

As a key activity of the home and office manager, delegation has both direct and derived benefits. Four of the most important are that delegation:

1. Increases effectiveness by extending what you can *do* to what you can *get done* through others;
2. Releases time for more important work;
3. Develops skills, initiative, knowledge and competence of staff/family members;
4. Ensures that decisions are made at the lowest possible level so that managers can maintain their effectiveness.

There are, however, many barriers to delegation. They include:

(a) The 'one man show' approach – thinking that you are really the only person who can carry out the task properly.
(b) No toleration of mistakes – delegation means you are giving another person the opportunity to carry out certain tasks and implicit in this is the possibility of failure. This does not mean that you accept repeated mistakes but rather that you train and develop the skills of people who are working for you.
(c) Urgency – leaving insufficient time to explain clearly what needs to be done.
(d) Upward delegation – being too ready with answers and fostering dependence of the people around you.

Decision-making

Indecision is a great time waster. The Pareto principle, named after the nineteenth-century Italian economist and sociologist Vilfredo Pareto, states that in general about 80 per cent of our results are achieved by a very significant 20 per cent of our efforts (see diagram page 92).

It is important to identify the high-value activities that will produce the desired results and to increase the amount of time spent on those activities. Consequently, the amount of time spent on less important activities is decreased. Also, most decisions can be made very quickly. Generally, this does not happen and too much time is spent agonising about who to ask to dinner or where to drive on Sunday and not enough time is given to making decisions that will have a major influence on our lives,

The Pareto Principle

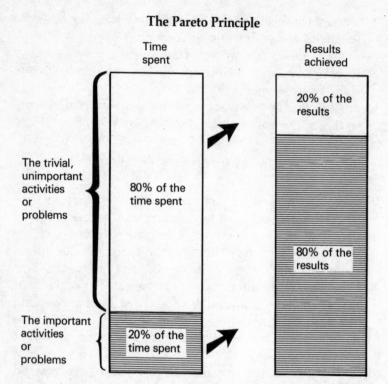

Time spent

Results achieved

The trivial, unimportant activities or problems

80% of the time spent

20% of the results

80% of the results

The important activities or problems

20% of the time spent

for example, choice of marriage partner or choice of training for future work.

Many people are indecisive because they fear making mistakes. Peter Drucker, the well-known management expert and writer, says that risk is implicit in all decisions and that too many people look on a decision as a problem rather than as an opportunity. They tend to settle for the safest solution with the least chance of failure even though it promises the lowest gain. Every decision is an attempt to balance gains, costs and risks. It is important both in business and personal development to take risks even though there is the possibility of failure.

Procrastination

Procrastination plagues all of us at times. We tend to delay difficult and unpleasant tasks – going to the dentist, starting that lengthy report, making that difficult phone call, cleaning the house windows. It's a natural tendency for people to want things to be easy, pleasant and hassle free. Life is not like that. Realities need to be faced and dealt with. How can we tackle those difficult things?

First, lists of goals are prepared and priorities established, but that is not enough. The important thing is to get started. If it is a major report, it may be something as simple as assembling files, paper, pens and references. If it is making a difficult phone call, it may mean jotting down the number, setting aside a specific time and making a few notes about what you are going to say and some possible replies. In these two examples the most important step is to get started. Many people defer a major task because they tell themselves it is too big or too difficult. Evidence shows that this type of self-talk decreases the chances of getting started. The fears and anxiety about the task will often significantly diminish once you actually come to grips with it.

The other important technique is to break the task down into a number of segments. Using the simple example of cleaning the house windows, if you set some time aside to do one room, then you've started and the remainder will not seem so daunting.

Deadlines
The setting of deadlines is another important method in overcoming procrastination and achieving objectives. When delegating a task or scheduling the steps to be taken towards an objective, set written deadlines for yourself and others. Deadlines work best when they are reached by agreement and are viewed as reasonable and fair.

Planning
The nuts and bolts of self-organisation are to plan in writing what you hope to achieve tomorrow, next week, next month and next year and this is done with the aid of a 'To do today' sheet, a 'Weekly' plan sheet, a 'Monthly' plan sheet and a 'Yearly' plan sheet. Examples of these are shown on pages 94–7.

Filling in these sheets does not mean that a crisis will be averted and that plans will not go amiss, but at least you will have a guide to return to when the crisis has passed.

Block out specific times during the day for leisure and relaxation, such as walking or just doing nothing. Time

Things to do today

Date:

Task	Priority A B C	Time needed	Done	Scheduled events
				8.00
				8.30
				9.00
				9.30
				10.00
				10.30
				11.00
				11.30
				12.00
				12.30
				1.00
				1.30
				2.00
				2.30
				3.00
				3.30
				4.00
				4.30
Phone calls	**Notes**			5.00
				5.30
				6.00
				Evening

Weekly work plan

Week commencing: ....

Priority	Projects	Mon	Tues	Wed	Thur	Fri
	1.					
	2.					
	3.					
	4.					
	5.					
	6.					
	7.					
	8.					

Notes

Monthly work plan

Month ....

Priority	Projects	To be done in week of	Follow-up dates	Done
	1.			
	2.			
	3.			
	4.			
	5.			
	6.			
	7.			
	8.			
	9.			
	10.			
	11.			
	12.			
Notes				

Yearly work plan

Year ....

Priority	Projects	To be done in month of	Follow-up dates	Done
	1.			
	2.			
	3.			
	4.			
	5.			
	6.			
	7.			
	8.			
	9.			
	10.			
	11.			
	12.			
	13.			
	14.			

management is not trying to do more things each day but deciding what is important in terms of your objectives and to stop doing things that are not important to you. One of the greatest skills of the home or office manager is to *learn to say 'No'*. (See also Chapter 4, Assertiveness Training.)

Tyranny of the urgent

Many of us at work and at home suffer from the so-called 'hurry' syndrome. We always seem to be rushing from one thing to another in our attempt to get things done. Often we start one task, partially finish it and go on to another. There seems to be an urgency about everything.

It is important for people to stop and analyse on paper, using a suitable form, what they are doing and whether their activities are accomplishing their objectives. Many tasks appear to be urgent or are requested by others and designated as urgent. But are they? If you are going to use your time more effectively, then in your own mind you need to establish:

1. What is urgent and important.
2. Important and not urgent.
3. Urgent and not important.
4. Not important and not urgent.

Deal with tasks in that order and many items that fall into categories 3 and 4 can be left.

Time logs

A very useful tool is to run a time log on yourself for a week whereby all the things you do are listed on a sheet. At the end of the week you analyse the amount of time you have spent on the various tasks and this can be compared with how much time you estimated you were spending on various activities. I will guarantee that it will be a shock to you.

So far I have been discussing self-organisation from a general perspective, that is, both at work and at home. I would now like to concentrate on self-organisation at work and then devote a major section to organisation at home. Many of the suggestions will be applicable to both, but I believe this division is the best way to present these ideas.

Managing at work

Blocking interruptions

One of the greatest obstacles to completing tasks is interruption. The average office manager is interrupted once every eight minutes. Time to think and plan is essential and if you allow unblocked interruptions then there is very little time for this. The main interruptions and methods to overcome them are:

Telephone calls

These need to be screened. Do not answer the phone automatically when it rings but, as far as possible, have calls answered by a receptionist, secretary or answering machine. The same applies at home when you need to set aside blocks of time to work on important projects, such as writing letters, applying for jobs, paying bills, having an important talk with your spouse or children. An unknown caller can interrupt and break an important chain of thought or discussion; therefore, literally pull out the plug on the phone or install an answering machine that you turn on at certain times when you do not wish to be disturbed.

Post

If you have a secretary or assistant have him or her open and sort the post. If you do it yourself, deal with it all at once, perhaps at the beginning or the end of each day. People who open post as soon as it arrives often find themselves distracted by what is in it.

Paper

An important objective for all of us to reduce the amount of time spent on paperwork. The *prime rule is to handle each piece of paper only once*. The following rules will cut paperwork time greatly:

- Dictate replies to letters into a dictation machine or handwrite an answer on the original letter, keep a photocopy and return the original with your reply. This is becoming an acceptable practice; some people even have a stamp saying, 'I hope you will understand the informality of this reply but it has enabled me to answer your letter much more quickly. Thank you.' This is then stamped on the original.

- Have a large wastepaper basket handy and throw out all unwanted mail as soon as it arrives.
- Read books like newspapers, skimming or only going to the chapters that seem of interest, then to the summary.
- Delegate other people to read reports, articles, etc, for you.
- Allow reading material to accumulate in a pile and then skim through it at suitable times.

Drop-in visitors
Establish a closed door policy as far as possible. Receive visitors by appointment. This does not mean that you are anti-social. You are quite happy to meet people at pre-arranged times, at tea breaks, at lunch or after work. Whether you are working at home or at the office and you want to finish the task at hand, a drop-in visitor can ruin your efforts. If an unexpected visitor gains entry during one of these important times, stand up and discuss the matter with him if you are in an office and escort him to the door. Do not keep comfortable chairs near your desk.

Waiting time
If you carry material such as plan sheets, drafts, articles or books, in your briefcase or bag, these can be worked on or read while waiting for an appointment or while waiting for or travelling on the train, bus or plane.

One task at a time
People have a tendency to get distracted very easily and there are tasks that we would prefer not to do. Procrastination is one problem that many of us face or we may start a task we may not particularly like and then something more attractive comes along and we start that, leaving task number one; the phone rings and interrupts us and soon we have four or five things going at once.

A fundamental principle for self-management is *to start and complete one task at a time*. Keep distracting material away from your desk. Try not to have your desk near open space where people walk or where there is a lot of activity and your thoughts can easily be diverted. Push yourself when you don't feel like getting started, and finish the task. Be sensible and set aside the most difficult and challenging tasks for that part of the day when *you know you are most alert and wide awake*. The morning is the best time for many people. Try to make sure the first hour of your working day is productive.

The secretary/manager team

I would like to cite two advertisements for secretaries I saw recently in the local paper:

1. 'WANTED: *A very special secretary* for a small insurance office. Must be prepared to run the messages, make the coffee, etc, and yet be mature enough to take responsibility for the day-to-day running of the office.'
2. 'We require a bright, enthusiastic secretary. We are involved in organising and running conferences and exhibitions on behalf of clients and ability to respond to people and cope with the varying daily circumstances and pressures is necessary. Word processing experience an advantage.'

These advertisements for secretaries are not unusual and suggest that a wide range of abilities and skills are required as well as a willingness to run messages and make tea.

The secretary's role

Management experts consider the secretary/manager team a most important unit. A good secretary can double the manager's worth to an organisation. A good secretary can facilitate a meeting, rescue you from an unwanted visitor and develop your small concept into an action plan.

What is a secretary? What should a secretary do? Certainly not everyone who is labelled 'secretary' actually functions as a secretary. Many people who are given this label have a single job function: typing, filing or greeting office visitors. Each of these activities is important to an organisation, but these functions alone do not fulfil the meaning of the word 'secretary'.

A definition that I saw recently, taken from a secretaries' association, is as follows: 'A secretary is an executive assistant who possesses a mastery of office skills, demonstrates the ability to assume responsibility without direct supervision, exercises initiative and judgement and makes decisions within the scope of assigned authority.' I use the feminine for secretaries as, at present, most are predominantly female, and the masculine for managers for the same reason.

Improving effectiveness

How can secretaries and managers improve their effectiveness?

First, communication is essential. The secretary and the manager must develop a good relationship so that they can speak to one another regularly about all things concerning the organisation and the office. Have at least one session a day with your secretary to plan what is going to be done, to let her know where you will be and what appointments, calls, letters are to be dealt with. Make out a 'To do today' list and share it with her.

Time management experts, including Dr Alec McKenzie, the author of *The Time Trap*, argue that secretaries can do much for the manager to save him time for the important managerial functions of planning, organising and controlling.

What a secretary can do

The secretary/personal assistant can help the manager by:

- Screening telephone calls, visitors and post.
- Dealing with many people herself on behalf of the manager. (I contact executives at all levels for many reasons and because I cannot make direct contact with executives, I am more than willing to discuss matters with their secretaries as I find that effective secretaries are excellent to deal with and the information or advice I obtain from them solves the problem. When I do reach the executive directly, after initial

contact with his secretary, we can negotiate or reach a decision in the minimum time.)

- Preparing papers for consideration, opening letters, sorting them on a priority basis so that the appropriate ones can be considered first by the manager.
- Organising the manager's desk, files and office layout.
- Drafting replies to routine correspondence.
- Composing letters using key ideas dictated by the manager.
- Providing advice and constructive crticism for the manager.
- Using a portable dictation machine so that letters, notes, ideas and reports can be dictated at the manager's convenience and valuable time is not lost by face to face dictation.

What a manager can do

As a manager you can:

- Listen to what your secretary says.
- Recognise that the secretary is an important member of your team: include her in meetings and development programmes so that she knows what is going on. (The more training staff receive the more effective performance you can expect, and will get.)
- Respect your secretary's time as much as your own and avoid interrupting her. Schedule your activities as much as possible in conjunction with hers.
- Provide training for your secretary wherever possible in relevant areas such as word processing, computer operation, management. Provide books and literature for her to upgrade her skills.
- Give clear instructions and take time to ensure that they are understood. Many managers are dominated by the 'tyranny of the urgent' and they leave very little time to explain what they are doing or how they want something done.
- Delegate to your secretary. Ask her what she feels she could do that you are now doing; you may be surprised. Don't feel you are the only one who can do all the marvellous things you are doing – this could yield valuable extra time for 'managing'. Ask her how she could manage your time

better. (Ideas from another person can be better than your own in many instances. The time involved is always worth the investment when it leads to more effective work.)

- Ask her to run a time log on you, that is, recording for one week in a diary all of your activities so that you can have an objective analysis of how you spend your time. This is recommended by all time management experts and invariably shocks the manager.

- Provide good working conditions for your secretary, ensuring that she has a suitably designed chair to prevent back problems. Lighting, desk, files should also be of good design quality and layout.

- Pay her what she is worth, because secretaries appear to be greatly undervalued. If it is not possible in cash, give her time off or other benefits.

- Treat her with dignity and respect. Provide support and do not abuse or embarrass her. (Many times one hears managers blaming their secretaries for reports not being ready on time, or for items being lost. This often means the manager failed to give clear instructions or set deadlines.)

- Encourage your secretary to take the initiative. She will make mistakes from time to time but that is how people learn. You will find that encouraging her and explaining what was wrong will pay handsome dividends in terms of how well you use your time.

Benefits

What are the benefits if you, as a manager, are willing to review the arrangements that exist between your secretary and yourself and implement at least some of the suggestions made?

I believe you will create a more effective management team. You will have more time to plan, think and organise your work. There will be increased motivation for both of you to get things done, and the atmosphere in your office will be better.

Dictation

A valuable skill to improve your time management is dictation, and a valuable tool you can acquire is a portable dictation unit.

Those of you who already use a portable recorder probably don't know how you got along without it, but studies show that as many as *four out of ten executives* write out their letters and memos by hand before turning them over for typing.

If you are one of these handwriters, try a little test to show yourself how much time you're wasting. How many words per minute can you write (or type – if that's what you've been doing)? Twenty? Thirty? Perhaps sixty if you're a pretty fair typist? Well, that's pretty slow when you consider that the spoken word comes out at about 150 words per minute.

If you're still dictating directly to your secretary, there is room for you to improve here too, since you're probably capable of speaking twice as fast as she is capable of taking down your words in shorthand.

So you can *more than quadruple* your speed if you are handwriting – or double it from dictating directly – just by switching to dictation equipment.

The convenience factor is important, too. The newer dictation machines are small and can be used in a car, on planes – kept with you at all times for note taking, delegating – even working on your expense report as it happens.

If your assistant or secretary rebels at the thought of dictating equipment, propose a test for several weeks. Some firms will lend you a test unit for a while before you purchase. Many secretaries find using the dictating machine a rewarding experience for them, too, since they can transcribe and type to suit their own daily schedules.

Dictation tricks

Pop tapes in and out
You can keep several tapes going at once – one for expenses, another for ideas, a third for correspondence and notes to people you delegate to. With the tiny cassettes, you can carry a number in a very small space. They're so small that you can easily post them back for transcribing if you are away for a while.

Keep a record of meetings
Sometimes you can eliminate the need for minutes of a meeting if you record it. That way, you will have a true record of what went on, but you needn't transcribe it unless a question comes up later. Make it known that you save these tapes for an agreed length of time, then erase them and reuse.

Have people report to you on tape
The Chief Operating Officer of a supermarket chain said, 'I used to waste time requiring written reports from staff, then reading them during valuable office or home hours. Now I ask them to dictate their reports, and I listen directly to their cassettes while I drive to work. This saves input and output time, and usually results in better understanding too!'

Record instructions for staff
You can transfer work to your staff easily by recording instructions on a cassette for them. For example, go through your post and explain on tape what needs to be done with each item. Then give the cassette and the post to your secretary and she can handle it.

If you're working late and want to leave some instructions for your staff, leave the 'To do' list on a cassette and your secretary or assistant can listen to it first thing in the morning. This is much quicker than scribbling out voluminous notes that may be too messy to be understood.

Doctors, lawyers and accountants who charge for their services by the hour find a special use for dictation.

A doctor explains his dictation time-saver. 'I use a portable cassette recorder to dictate my findings and recommendations just after seeing a patient. The dictation saves me time and gives me other advantages: I get the work done while the facts are fresh in my mind.'

Learn to dictate effectively
If you're a novice at dictation, you may need some pointers on how to dictate effectively. There are books devoted wholly to this subject, but here you'll find some ideas that may be enough to

point you in the right direction. The following guidelines will help you keep on track when you dictate. I suggest you make a poster or card with these points on it and keep it in front of you while dictating.

The 'Preparation' column below refers to activities before you actually start dictating. First, jot down the objectives about which you are writing, and then a brief outline that may contain just key words. It is also important to have at hand references that you are going to cite or quote from. Then set yourself sufficient time to dictate.

The 'Execution' column below refers to things to do once you start dictating. First, you need to put clear instructions on the tape about the letterhead, anything special regarding typing and when it is to be done. You then dictate distinctly in a relaxed fashion, spelling any words you think may be necessary, such as proper names, towns or technical terms and punctuating as much as possible. It is also useful to indicate the time and date of each dictation.

Dictation

Preparation	Execution
Objectives	Instructions
Outline	Distinct speech
References	Relax
Take time	Spelling

Managing at home

This is usually done by women, and for those who are working outside the home as well, managing the home can be very difficult. It is a complex responsibility and I have attempted a job description:

1. Resolution of family conflicts.
2. Assisting with children's homework, hobbies and teaching social skills.
3. Balancing the budget.
4. Buying and transporting food supplies.
5. Buying and maintaining family clothing, including washing and ironing.
6. Cooking.
7. Maintaining and repairing the home including appliances, furniture, toys.
8. Chauffeuring children.
9. Looking after pets.

The key to managing the home is *effective delegation*. Delegation means taking the time to train people to do things around the home and to show them that they are responsible for their actions. It is important to remember that *perfectionism* is a major barrier to effective delegation. Typical self-defeating thoughts for many women are:

- 'Only I can do that properly.'
- 'I must have a perfect house with beautifully cooked meals.'
- 'My children must succeed at all they do.'
- 'When my expectations of any or all of the above aren't met I am a failure.'

It is fine to have goals and strong preferences, but as soon as they turn into *demands* they generally cause anxiety.

A list of time-wasters is shown opposite and the similarities between the middle-management supervisors and home managers and between time-wasting at work and at home are striking. Telephone interruptions, drop-in visitors, ineffective delegation, attempting too much, no daily planning and failure to set goals and deadlines are common to both.

Composite time-waster profile
(rankings by frequency)

Time-waster	Middle management supervisors	Women at home
Telephone	1	2
Ineffective delegation	1	1
Drop-in visitors	3	9
Crisis management/Shifting priorities/Firefighting	4	6
Lack of objectives, priorities, daily plan	5	5
Attempting too much	6	3
Cluttered desk/Personal disorganisation	7	12
Meetings	8	17
Procrastination	9	8
Inability to say No	10	10
Chauffeuring children	–	4
Ineffective communication	11	24
Inadequate/untrained staff	12	13
Personnel with problems	13	–
Incomplete information	13	–
Leaving tasks unfinished	15	7

Work area and record-keeping

A work area at home is vital, be it a desk (which is strongly recommended) or a table top where planning can take place and where supplies such as memo pads, 'To do today' sheets, files, pens, pencils, clips and folders are kept. A simple filing system is needed in every home to keep all the legal and household-related documents in order and easy to locate. This prevents the unnecessary frustration of never being able to find your National Health number for health insurance or locate last year's tax return or your TV licence.

Six categories of document are suggested:

1. *Personal documents.* These include key family records such as wills, birth, marriage and death certificates. Also included are passports, school reports, diplomas and social security records.
2. *Property records.* Papers relating to the house, such as deeds, mortgage documents and a record of capital improvements, and a household inventory should be filed.
3. *Financial records.* Needing safe keeping are any stocks and bonds, records for pension and profit-sharing plans, bank account information and any retail credit and hire-purchase contracts.
4. *Insurance records.* The policies may be for life, accident, public liability, car, and so on; keep any receipts.
5. *Health records.* An up-to-date health record is an invaluable resource to have. This record should include such items as insurance information and receipts, immunisation and infectious disease records and any other significant infor-mation relating to family illness.
6. *Tax records.* Not only should you keep copies of your annual tax return forms, you also need to file all relevant receipts plus any other verification of your tax payments.

Although most items can be kept at home, there are some that are best kept in a safe deposit box at a bank. This will ensure safety from fire and theft of those items that would be difficult, if not impossible, to replace. Such things as birth and marriage certificates, deeds, wills, household inventory and important contracts should be kept in a safe deposit box with copies at home. Alternatively, copies of these documents can be kept at work or at a relative's home.

The six categories of document listed are divided into active files and should include:

- Tax documents
- Unpaid bills
- Paid bill receipts
- Current bank statements
- National Insurance records
- Employment records
- Health and social security benefits information
- Credit card information
- Insurance policies
- Copies of wills
- Family health records
- Appliance manuals and guarantees
- Receipts for items under warranty
- Education information
- Inventory of safe deposit box, key and photocopies of documents
- Loan statements
- Loan payment records
- Receipts of expensive items still being paid for

Don't let paperwork pile up at home. Look over post, school reports and other items marked for your attention the day they arrive. If they can't be dealt with immediately, deal with them before the end of the week. When you do deal with accumulated paper, decide at that time what items are to be filed, thrown out or marked for further attention.

Paying the bills
This should be organised as efficiently as possible.

1. Whenever you receive a bill put it with the others as it will not usually need to be paid immediately.

2. Once every two weeks or month balance the cheque book and sort the bills to be paid if all can't be paid at once.
3. Retain cheque stubs for correct reconciliation with the bank statement when it arrives.

Message board

The kitchen is the main place for much activity in the home and a message board is best located in the kitchen or somewhere nearby so that instructions, reminders, lists can be placed on it. A family calendar is also best placed in the kitchen on the board. Train children to leave notes when they go out. Ask them to specify their destination and telephone number, time of return and other important information.

Cooking

1. Delegate as much as possible and train others to prepare meals so that they can be assigned the responsibility of preparing a certain number of meals per week.
2. Buy acceptable precooked meals that can be frozen and stored.
3. Eat out at inexpensive restaurants either by yourself, with the family and/or friends and think of this as money spent on 'quality time' where you can relax, have pleasant conversations or discuss problems in a non-threatening atmosphere. I recommend to my married clients with communication problems that they do this regularly.

Shopping

1. As far as possible shop for groceries, meat and all food and household items once a week only.
2. Experiment to find the least crowded day and time.
3. Keep a pad and pencil in the kitchen for a supplementary shopping list – jot down buying needs as they appear.
4. Speed up the pre-shopping list by drawing up a master list of all the food and household items you buy at least once a month. Take copies and you can prepare a list for each week simply by ticking off the items needed at that time. Refine

this technique to save a little more time by conforming your list to the supermarket's layout.

5. Buy in multiple quantities to save time running to the shop regularly for each item.
6. If possible, consider using a shopping service.

Cleaning

1. Be prepared to spend money on services such as cleaning if both adult partners in the family are working. This will leave time for relaxation and for other activities. If this is not possible, then delegate and train family members to make their beds, dust, vacuum and be responsible for their own rooms. Shared living areas, such as the lounge and dining areas, need to be cleaned regularly so make a clear, written rota of who is to do it.
2. Have all cleaning materials in one box or bucket so that they can be easily moved from room to room but returned to one place and that everyone knows where that is. Again, schedule tasks as far as possible in advance.

Washing and ironing

1. Train people in the house to be able to sort clothes and use the washing machine.
2. Have two laundry baskets, one for whites and one for coloured.
3. Make adult members of the household responsible for their own washing and ironing.
4. Never hang up a garment that isn't ready to wear. When you take off an article that needs cleaning or repairing, set it aside until you can take care of it. This saves time when you are at your busiest – your early morning minutes seem to evaporate as you get things together for a day at the office. The same applies to children's clothes.

Appointments

1. On the first day of each month, remind yourself about weddings, birthdays and parties coming up.

2. Buy all the required gifts, wrapping paper, cards, etc, on one shopping trip.
3. Get to know the shops that will giftwrap purchases and deliver them on telephone instructions.
4. When you make an appointment, such as with the hairdresser or the dentist, explain that your time is limited because of work commitments. You are then more likely to get special consideration and faster service. In return, don't cancel at the last minute.

Service and repair people

1. Keep a file with the names and telephone numbers of key service people.
2. It is worthwhile developing a good relationship with a plumber, electrician and other handymen. By doing so, one call will bring help quickly for that sudden emergency or breakdown.

Review existing arrangements about who will do what in the house on a regular basis during relaxed times, for example immediately after dinner. It is clearly only fair that the tasks associated with maintaining a home be shared among family members who live in and benefit from it.

It is worth spending time training and giving clear instructions about tasks in the home. Once an individual family member has mastered a task and realised it is their responsibility, many hours will be saved.

Commitment and low frustration tolerance

Self-organisation, as stated earlier in this chapter, is about getting things done, that is, changing the A in the ABC model. It requires planning and persistence. It means analysing your goals, setting priorities and examining how you use that precious recource – your time. Everyone has 168 hours each week. The question we frequently need to ask is how we use them.

There are things we can change or try to change in our lives. If we decide to work on a problem, turn it into a challenge and attack it systematically, we are likely to get some results. Remember, problems are rarely black and white. If our first objective is not achieved, there are almost always alternatives which may be possible with some compromise.

Low frustration tolerance (LFT) is one of the great obstacles to human achievement. Push yourself hard when trying something new. Keep filling in your 'To do today' sheet each day for at least a month – don't stop after a week. When it is thrust upon you, welcome frustration as a learning experience and your tolerance will increase, and you can expect to deal with the next difficult situation more effectively.

Other people will value you, learn from you, and even love you because of your self-organisation.

Twelve steps to successful time management

1. Develop a personal philosophy of time – what time means to you and how time relates to your life.
2. Clarify your objectives. Put them in writing. Then set your priorities. Make sure you're getting what you really want out of life.
3. Set at least one major objective each day and achieve it. Conquer procrastination. Learn to do it now.
4. Record a time log periodically to analyse how you use your time, and keep bad time habits out of your life.
5. Analyse everything you do in terms of your objectives. Find out what you do, when you do it, why you do it. Ask yourself what would happen if you didn't do it. If the answer is nothing, then stop doing it.
6. Eliminate at least one time waster from your life each week.
7. Plan your time. Write out a plan for each week, each month, each year; ask yourself what you hope to accomplish and what you will need to do to achieve those results.
8. Make a 'To do' list every day. Be sure it includes your daily objectives, priorities, and time estimates, not just random activities.

9. Make sure that the first hour of your working day is productive.
10. Institute a quiet hour in your day – a block of uninterrupted time for your most important tasks.
11. Develop the habit of finishing what you start. Don't jump from one thing to another, leaving a string of unfinished tasks behind you.
12. Take time for yourself – time to relax, time to live.

References

A Lakein, *How to Get Control of your Time and Your Life*, Gower (1985)

R A McKenzie, *The Time Trap*, McGraw-Hill, (1975)

A MacKenzie and K Waldo, *About Time: A Woman's Guide to Time Management*, McGraw-Hill (1981)

M E Douglass and D N Douglass *Manage your Time, Manage Your Work, Manage Yourself*, Amacom, USA (1980)

P Drucker, *The Effective Executive*, Pan Books (1970)

P Drucker, *Management in Turbulent Times*, Pan Books (1981)

RET Self-Help Form

(A) **ACTIVATING EVENTS:** thoughts, or feelings that happened just before I felt emotionally disturbed or acted self-defeatingly: _____

_____

(B) BELIEFS – IRRATIONAL BELIEFS (IBs) leading to my CONSEQUENCE (emotional disturbance or self-defeating behaviour). Circle all that apply to these ACTIVATING EVENTS (A).	(D) DISPUTES for each circled IRRATIONAL BELIEF. Examples: 'Why MUST I do very well?' 'Where is it written that I am a BAD PERSON?' 'Where is the evidence that I MUST be approved or accepted?'
1. I MUST do well or very well!	....
2. I am a BAD OR WORTHLESS PERSON when I act weakly or stupidly.	....
3. I MUST be approved or accepted by people I find important!	....
4. I am a BAD UNLOVABLE PERSON if I get rejected.	....
5. People MUST treat me fairly and give me what I NEED!	....
6. People who act immorally are undeserving, ROTTEN PEOPLE!	....
7. People MUST live up to my expectations or it is TERRIBLE!	....
8. My life MUST have few major hassles or troubles.	....
9. I CAN'T STAND really bad things or very difficult people!	....
10. It's AWFUL or HORRIBLE when major things don't go my way!	....
11. I CAN'T STAND IT when life is really unfair!	....
12. I NEED to be loved by someone who matters to me a lot!	....

(C) CONSEQUENCE or CONDITION: disturbed feeling or self-defeating behaviour that I produced and would like to change: _____

_____

_____

(E) EFFECTIVE RATIONAL BELIEFS (RBs) to replace my IRRATIONAL BELIEFS (IBs). Examples: _'I'd PREFER to do very well but I don't HAVE TO.' 'I am a PERSON WHO acted badly, not a BAD PERSON.' 'There is no evidence that I HAVE TO be approved, though I would LIKE to be.'_

_____

....
....
....
....
....
....
....
....
....
....
....
....
....
....
....
....
....
....
....
....
....
....
....
....
....
....
....
....
....
....
....
....

(B) BELIEFS – IRRATIONAL BELIEFS (IBs) leading to my CONSEQUENCE (emotional disturbance or self-defeating behaviour). Circle all that apply to these ACTIVATING EVENTS (A).	(D) DISPUTES for each circled IRRATIONAL BELIEF. Examples: *'Why MUST I do very well?'* *'Where is it written that I am a BAD PERSON?'* *'Where is the evidence that I MUST be approved or accepted?'*
13. I NEED a good deal of immediate gratification and HAVE TO feel miserable when I don't get it!	....
Additional irrational beliefs:	
14.	
15.	
16.	
17.	
18.	

(F) FEELINGS and BEHAVIOUR PATTERNS I experienced after arriving at my EFFECTIVE RATIONAL BELIEFS: _____

....
....
....
....
....
....
....
....
....
....
....
....
....
....
....
....
....
....
....
....
....
....
....
....
....
....
....
....
....
....

I will work hard to repeat my effective rational beliefs forcefully to myself on many occasions so that I can make myself less disturbed now and act less self-defeatingly in the future.

Rational Statements for you to cut out and keep in your wallet or on your bulletin board

Stop catastrophising!
The worst rarely happens.

So what if ....
....

I would like the world to be
a perfect place all the time
but I cannot make it perfect, so
sometimes I will be treated unfairly.

There is generally no gain
without pain.

Take calculated risks
if you wish to enjoy life more.

Because I failed at a particular
activity does not mean I am a
failure as a person.
I can learn from my mistakes.

Demands are not healthy for me.
It is in my interest to change
demands into strong preferences.

I don't like frustration but
I can damn well stand it.